BUSINESS NETWORKING

The term 'networking' can mean very different things in different contexts: formal organisational structures, personal or career development, or a technique for increasing sales. This is an approachable book which brings together the basics of all these meanings, underpinned by an overview of multiple theoretical models that support the various approaches to networking.

Drawing on mainstream models in the fields of marketing, employability, innovation and organisational studies, *Business Networking* provides an integrated overview of the process and structure of networking across a range of contexts. Synthesising theory with practice, features include examples and viewpoints from a range of networking practitioners in each chapter, presented in their own words, as well as chapter summaries and reflective questions. Networking is considered a key skill for students, entrepreneurs and practitioners and, given the explosion of opportunities brought by the digital age for individuals and organisations to operate within a broad and global network, an introduction to maximising the benefits is timely.

This book should be recommended reading for a broad range of postgraduate courses, from relationship marketing and entrepreneurship skills to employability and degree apprenticeship programmes. It should also be useful for reflective practitioners looking to expand and utilise their networks effectively.

Catherine O'Sullivan has a long career history in workforce development. This includes supporting medical students at the University of Leeds to use networking skills as part of their career planning. Formerly, she ran a large NHS innovation network and has published in the areas of professional and continuing education, leadership and innovation. She is a co-author of *Creative Arts Marketing*, 3rd edition (Routledge, 2017).

Terry O'Sullivan is Senior Lecturer in Management at The Open University Business School. He was lead educator on the FutureLearn Massive Open Online Course *Business Fundamentals: Effective Networking* studied by tens of thousands of learners across the world, and is also a co-author of *Creative Arts Marketing*, 3rd edition (Routledge, 2017).

BUSINESS NETWORKING

Innovation and Ideas in
Theory and Practice

Catherine O'Sullivan and Terry O'Sullivan

LONDON AND NEW YORK

First published 2022
by Routledge
2 Park Square, Milton Park, Abingdon, Oxon OX14 4RN

and by Routledge
605 Third Avenue, New York, NY 10158

Routledge is an imprint of the Taylor & Francis Group, an informa business

© 2022 Catherine O'Sullivan and Terry O'Sullivan

The right of Catherine O'Sullivan and Terry O'Sullivan to be identified as authors of this work has been asserted by them in accordance with sections 77 and 78 of the Copyright, Designs and Patents Act 1988.

All rights reserved. No part of this book may be reprinted or reproduced or utilised in any form or by any electronic, mechanical, or other means, now known or hereafter invented, including photocopying and recording, or in any information storage or retrieval system, without permission in writing from the publishers.

Trademark notice: Product or corporate names may be trademarks or registered trademarks, and are used only for identification and explanation without intent to infringe.

British Library Cataloguing-in-Publication Data
A catalogue record for this book is available from the British Library

Library of Congress Cataloging-in-Publication Data
Names: O'Sullivan, Catherine, 1956 December 5- author. | O'Sullivan, Terry, 1957– author.
Title: Business networking : innovation and ideas in theory and practice / Catherine O'Sullivan and Terry O'Sullivan.
Description: New York, NY : Routledge, 2022. | Includes bibliographical references and index.
Subjects: LCSH: Business enterprises—Computer networks. | Internet.
Classification: LCC HD30.37 .O868 2022 (print) |
LCC HD30.37 (ebook) | DDC 338.70285—dc23
LC record available at https://lccn.loc.gov/2021019154
LC ebook record available at https://lccn.loc.gov/2021019155

ISBN: 978-0-367-46027-3 (hbk)
ISBN: 978-0-367-46028-0 (pbk)
ISBN: 978-1-003-02654-9 (ebk)

DOI: 10.4324/9781003026549

Typeset in Bembo
by codeMantra

For Sarah, Tim, Katy, Abbey and Joely, their partners and their children: with our love

CONTENTS

List of figures		*ix*
About the authors		*xi*
	Introduction	1
1	Networking: innovation and ideas	7
2	The ethics of networking	31
3	Networking across organisational boundaries	53
4	Networking for business growth	77
5	Networking for social change	96
6	Networking and personal growth	119
Index		*143*

FIGURES

1.1	Anticipated benefits of networking	15
1.2	The network-IN model	19
3.1	Establishing and developing cross-sector health innovation collaborations	58
3.2	Establishing and developing cross-sectoral health innovation collaborations (modified)	67
3.3	The network-IN model (repeated)	68
3.4	Network stakeholder model	70
3.5	Network saliency model	71
4.1	A model for managing in networks	84
4.2	Resource-based view of strategy	87
5.1	A simplified version of the social change model applied to networking	114
6.1	Imagined personal network 1	120
6.2	Imagined personal network 2	121

ABOUT THE AUTHORS

Catherine O'Sullivan currently manages a portfolio career in health and care workforce development, with a particular interest in leadership and innovation. She works part-time at the medical school of the University of Leeds and at the University of York, and for two statutory regulators.

Prior to that, she established and led the Thames Valley Health Innovation and Education Cluster known as The Knowledge Team, securing its legacy as a major catalyst for change and improvement across the NHS in the Thames Valley region. Previous roles include that of Chief Operating Officer in a London university, commissioner of NHS workforce education and learning in the West Midlands, and extended secondments for both the Department of Health and the Department of Education and Skills. She started her working life in accountancy and was the first Director of Finance of the West Yorkshire Playhouse, now Leeds Playhouse, after an earlier role at the Royal Opera House.

Catherine read English at St. Anne's College, Oxford, and later gained an MSc in Public Service Management and a professional doctorate in education (EdD), researching into a lifelong interest – learning for, from and in work. She has published and presented extensively in the areas of professional and continuing education, leadership and innovation. Other titles include *Creative Arts Marketing* and *Reshaping Herbal Medicine: Knowledge, Education and Professional Culture*.

Dr Terry O'Sullivan is a Senior Lecturer in Management in The Open University Business School. Terry's professional experience includes fast-moving consumer goods and theatre marketing. His interest in networking stems from curiosity about how people market themselves to colleagues and employers (existing and potential). He became a full-time academic in 2002, and a Senior Fellow of the Higher Education Academy in 2019. His teaching experience

xii About the authors

includes acting as lead educator on the highly successful FutureLearn MOOC 'Business Fundamentals: Effective Networking', as well as devising and delivering courses on strategy and marketing at undergraduate and postgraduate levels. Terry's research has appeared in journals such as *Journal of Marketing Management* and *Consumption Markets and Culture* and he is co-author of another popular Routledge text: *Creative Arts Marketing*, now in its third edition.

INTRODUCTION

The purpose of this brief introduction is to set out our reasons for writing this book, and give a short overview of how we approached the task. We discuss the research approach we took to the book, and discuss some of the limitations to that and therefore the agenda for future research in this area. Finally, we offer you, the reader, some ideas for how you might best use this book to support your own networking interests.

Why another book on networking?

Our interest in networking began with practitioner work we were doing in our professional lives and in supporting the students with whom we work, particularly with regard to their employability skills. In the approximate time period between 2010 and 2020, we both found ourselves in network leadership roles: one leading a health innovation network of the kind discussed in Chapter 3 and the other putting together Massive Open Online Courses (MOOCs) on employability skills with networking a hot topic area. We found a gap in the literature on networking, with no generalist texts that took a broad-brush approach to networking as a mainstream work-related skill, crossing disciplinary and professional boundaries. There is a wealth of top-quality academic research into networking that deserves to be more widely known – an important reason for writing this book. And while there are a number of 'how to' skills-based books on networking, these by and large focus on networking to improve sales rather than exploring broader motivations for networking. Our own interest in particular is in networking as a vehicle for spreading new ideas, enabling individuals to extend their repertoire of personal and professional ways-of-knowing and to support innovation through the cross-fertilisation of knowledge from very different epistemologies.

DOI: 10.4324/9781003026549-1

2 Introduction

Our empirical research

To a large degree, this book should be viewed as a reader into research into networks and networking. What we hope to do is to introduce seminal texts, known in specific disciplinary areas, into a wider and more generalist readership. We hope this will inspire at least some of our readers to follow up references that interest them that they first meet in these pages.

We did however carry out an initial survey into people's motivations for networking ($n = 338$), followed up by in-depth interviews into 5% ($n = 16$) of survey respondents exploring their various networking experiences in some depth, beginning with the seemingly simple question – 'what does networking mean to you?' (Box 0.1).

BOX 0.1 OVERVIEW OF OUR RESEARCH STUDY

Abstract

As online opportunities proliferate to complement face-to-face networking, refreshing our understanding of attitudes to networking, and the variety of networking behaviour (across business, self-development and community contexts), is a timely undertaking.

This exploratory project combines an online survey of people who engage in networking activity with follow-up telephone interviews to test an emerging model of how and why people network in a range of contexts.

Participants

The population targeted is all adults who engage in networking behaviour. We will therefore be relying on convenience sampling sharing the survey link widely with business and professional associations, colleagues, university alumni, personal contacts and social media platforms. We are aiming for international responses through ensuring the survey link is available in countries other than the UK. This should ensure a measure of diversity in responses. The survey will be available in English only, which has the disadvantage of limiting responses to anglophone participants.

Recruitment

Potential participants will be identified through our reasoned assumptions as to their likely interest in and practice of networking. Professional associations and personal contacts, colleagues and alumni will be the starting point. While access to any of these starting points will depend on personal contacts

---

Introduction **3**

and leads, the snowballing process should mitigate any preponderance of personal or professional links to the researchers as more respondents come on board. Any danger of coercion or conflict of interest will be mitigated by emphasising the voluntary nature of participation in invitations and information about the research, by keeping the research instruments as user-friendly as possible and by guaranteeing anonymity in any published material which draws on the research.

Consent

The online survey opens on a page introducing the survey and giving information on Principal Investigator, alternative contact at Open University (OU), date after which consent cannot be withdrawn, assurance that data will be stored securely and retained according to OU data retention policy and confirmation of ethics approval. Additional consent will be sought when arranging telephone interviews with participants who have provided their emails for this purpose.

Extracted from full approved application for ethics approval: Open University HREC 3579

Viewpoint 0.1 What does networking mean to you?

Linking up with people who might share an interest to exchange ideas, build on thoughts, make connections and links in terms of sharing pieces of work, experience, expertise. (Person 1)

In essence, as I go through my kind of career adventure, as it were, along the way I meet interesting people and I have interesting conversations with them; and out of that will often fall insights or inspirations or ideas that then can provoke further interesting conversations (Person 2)

I understand it that networking is a term which is used in business circumstances more really than in purely social circumstances, and it means keeping in touch with the people in your field of activity (Person 3)

The more instrumentalist meaning is to meet people and make contacts that potentially are useful, and then revisit those contacts when necessary. Or putting people together if it seems that it might be beneficial to both parties. The less instrumentalist view is more about getting to know more people and be able in the future, review; to come back to those people in terms of exchanging ideas, developing thoughts and developing new things (Person 4)

It was a very cynical, you know, occupational pursuit and I hated it; kind of knowing that I had to... I couldn't be myself (Person 5)

4 Introduction

From our research, we have developed our own model, the network-IN model of networking practice, which is presented in Chapter 1 and discussed throughout the book. More importantly for the reader, we also obtained a variety of interesting vignettes and case studies of practitioner experience, which we use throughout to illuminate and problematise some of the more theoretical ideas explored in the book.

Limitations on the research

We acknowledge that all the main work in this book has almost exactly coincided with the global pandemic, COVID-19. Unfortunately, this has restricted our ability to the fieldwork we had planned, particularly in relation to work we had hoped to do in Africa. For this reason, we have not discussed the question of how networking in practice may vary in different cultural contexts – a huge topic and one which is really beyond the scope of this short book. In the Viewpoints, we offer just a couple of insights into this and identify it as an interesting field for further research.

Viewpoint 0.2 Does networking vary in different cultures?

I think also it's a generational thing. I can't speak for the current generation; I don't know exactly how they position themselves in terms of their Russianness because for me Russianness, in my case, is very much merged with the Soviet past. So how things used to operate in the command-and-control economy, how things were very much regimented. Breaking away from that is an important factor. (Person A)

The thing that I would say is that in Singapore, hierarchies are more important so I would become... or I will be perhaps a lot more deferential to an elderly or an older person in my emotional network, of which I had some from church in Singapore. There were some elderly ladies who I liked very much, actually they were so, so lovely, but I would be a lot more deferential than I would perhaps be to a similar person in Austria. (Person B)

But, in China, it's normally family friends who will recommend one another, even for a job opportunity. So, it's more like a personal circle/life circle rather than a professional working circle. In Asian cultures that connexion is, is cut like a wild mind map. Everything's connected together. So even if one's personal smaller family circle doesn't have any reference, it's more through friends and then friends' friends, then friends' friends' friends. So, it is kind of like everything is connected. (Person C)

I've become very conscious of not wanting to make sweeping statements about the US versus the UK, or the US as a country as a whole, because I live on the west coast which is very different, you know. (Person D)

A second impact of the pandemic was the discussion from most respondents about how they felt about working online. Much of this did not directly relate to networking so is not included. More relevantly, some respondents hazarded guesses into the extent to which either industry-based formal networking may have changed for ever or alternatively posited a view that life would soon return to the previous normal as networking is essentially a deeply social activity. As time alone will tell, we excluded much of this interesting debate from these pages as we feel it is too narrowly relevant to the present minute.

More general limitations to our research, and indeed to the scope of this book, are discussed in Chapter 1. These can largely be summarised in the conundrum; it all depends on what you mean by networking. While we offer a specific definition and explain our exclusion choices, we emphasise here that these remain choices. Our wish is to write an eclectic introduction to networking. However, on the grounds of practicality and word length, we have had to set some boundaries. We encourage readers to define networking for themselves and to follow up actively their interest beyond these pages.

Finally, on first reading the Viewpoints, it may appear our respondents' reported speech does not sound to you wholly genuine. In the interests of readability, we have tidied up reported speech, missed out most of the hesitations and gaps and completed fractured sentences. Beyond that, we have not changed the sense of what was said, and thank our respondents for their time and their insights. Our particular hope is that some of the new material we are offering here, perhaps particularly around the ethics of networking, may start a new interdisciplinary moment in network research.

How to use this book

We do not see this as the kind of book that is read from cover to cover. Depending on your current networking experience and practice, we suggest you use the book selectively. We hope most readers will look at Chapters 1 and 2, as these explain our approach and its limitations, offer a definition, and introduce our Network-In model which we use as a loose framework for the book. Chapter 2 looks at the ethics of networking which we believe is generally a gap in both theory and practice at the moment. Those who are involved in, or possibly lead, managed or more formal networks will find Chapters 3 and 4 most useful. Anyone who is working in local communities, bringing people together for mutual support or to design social change, will see that Chapter 5 covers those themes. Finally, Chapter 6 covers the more traditional areas relating to employability – personal learning and growth and career development.

There are some overarching themes covered in all chapters to a greater or lesser degree. Ethics, as mentioned above, is one of them. A second one is innovation and the ability of networking to expose people to ideas and approaches that are new to them and thus extend their personal and professional boundaries. Throughout, we draw extensively on the research literature in the hope that people will read further into empirical ideas that are maybe identified and investigated in very different arenas to the ones in which you live and work.

6 Introduction

Viewpoint 0.3 Innovation and ideas from networking

Certainly, in the corporate world, it's kind of the ability to build a network or a group of people with common ideas, my goals, my ways of working: but also, to be able to reach out to that network if there's something you're not sure of, that you'd like to look for a subject matter expert, I guess. So, if I think about my network, it's probably quite a wide range of people from different backgrounds, even different countries because I work for a global organisation; so, for me it's critical that my network has got a global reach on it.

I mean, in the roles that I'm in, I don't really have anything to do with the sales side of it; so my networks are about innovation and opportunities for innovation. So obviously yes, it does map up on to chances of sales. But it's more about using just such a wide range of people to be able to really think about innovative things; and risks as well, risks that people might come across that you might not have considered.

A lot of the work I do crosses… we are a global organisation and my role is global. For me to be able to get people on board with the specific projects or improvement activities, I really need to understand what that looks like to them and whether there is a cultural difference. Sometimes I need to rephrase things, think about the language I use with some of the people. I work with, in, different countries, they have different needs. But I've learned along the way, so that sometimes I will reach out to people within that network to test my understanding of something before I deliver it, and check that it's culturally sensitive as well.

Finally, each chapter suggests the practical application of the theoretical ideas discussed in the chapter. We are interested largely in the practice of networking and hope to encourage individual readers to think more about their networking strategy and approach. Each chapter contains a number of Viewpoints and verbatim quotations from our interviews, which may confirm, challenge or illuminate a theoretical point under discussion in the main chapter text. Theory offers insights into practice and, conversely, practice extends and problematises our understanding of theory. This is the reason for offering insights from our research respondents, particularly in the extended Networking Narratives that conclude each chapter followed by discussion questions. By thinking about the perspective of another, we hope you will be encouraged to consider these kinds of ideas in your own context, and thus to extend and improve your networking practice.

1

NETWORKING

Innovation and ideas

Introduction

The purpose of this chapter is to consider what we mean by networking, and to think about the different ways by which networking may advance ideas and new ways of working. Issues and concepts introduced here will be considered and discussed further in later chapters. Thus, the chapter acts as an overview of some of the salient characteristics, issues and problems of networking in theory and practice.

A significant issue in writing this book is agreeing exactly what networking is and what it is not (Möller and Halinen, 2017). Therefore, this chapter offers our definition of networking, and goes onto discussing the implications and challenges that arise from our definition and the boundaries to what we include within it. Although the term 'networking' is in wide general use, it can mean different things to different people. While we wish to encompass as broad a definition as possible in order to facilitate a discussion of what 'networking' comprises, we do need to start somewhere. In later chapters, we will problematise some of the ideas contained in our definition and discuss some of its limitations.

Our definition derives in part from our extensive review of the many literatures on networking, which are discussed further below as one of the challenges that arise in this area. We will explain why we consider it neither possible nor desirable to attempt one single theoretical insight into this broad topic. We have also carried out empirical research into the experiences of individuals networking in practice. These enquiries have given rise to our model of Network-IN, which we introduce below and are summarised in our definition. Our definition lays emphasis on both the purpose and the anticipated benefits of networking as an intentional practice; reflecting the ways in which respondents discussed the topic; and what we believe to be the main interest of readers of this book.

DOI: 10.4324/9781003026549-2

8 Networking: innovation and ideas

Viewpoint 1.1 Why I network

I would like to think that I'm in a lot of networks with people different to me; but I suspect that if you were to view them objectively, they are probably all similar. But there are networks of people – for example, using WhatsApp, I have a group with all the doctors I went to Sandhurst with. We share a common ground of a shared experience six or seven years ago, and now there are 40 people spread across different job roles – doctors, medical surgeons, GPs – in different parts of the UK and overseas. That is a very helpful source of information; be it about the name and contact details of someone I need to speak to, or how to manage a certain medical problem or what the latest update is in a certain area.

Definition

Our definition of networking is:

> The purposeful building and managing of relationships to grow or improve business or services; to spread and promote ideas and ideals; or to support personal and career development.

This definition requires some amplification and explanation.

First, the word 'purposeful' is important in our definition. The concern of this book is intentional networking. While it is undeniably true that important contacts can come from accidental meetings in a pub or at a party, our concern is with those who knowingly are or intend to be involved in networking for one of the purposes we outline. We are therefore excluding activity which mainly exists for a social or leisure reason, and are confining our definition to a conscious act with an intended end. In its broadest terms, we can say that networks are collectives of individuals around a common purpose. It may be that the end result is not defined, or understood in any detail, prior to starting networking. The potential benefits of networking are discussed in more detail in later sections below, when we set out our network model.

Second, the notion that networking is a purposeful activity implies some management of the process on the part of the individual or the organisation engaging in it. This will vary depending on the kinds of networks which are involved – some may be formal and managed while others may be very local and personal. These latter networks will tend to be managed by the individual personally. Whatever the kind of network involved, it won't be sustained without some effort. Given that it takes time to build relationships, the various parties involved will need to commit time and possibly resource to that effort (Tamarit et al., 2018). This is made explicit in the phrase we use: 'building and managing'.

Third, while our definition may seem to imply that there are three reasons why people engage in networking and that these are mutually exclusive, in reality this is not the case. Individuals or organisations may start networking for one reason and find it leads to something else (Van Baalen et al., 2005). Equally, things change over time and the nature of networking activity, being relatively informal, makes it peculiarly able to adapt or morph as the individuals within the network change, develop new interests or face new challenges and opportunities. While we wanted to make it clear that all these forms of networking fall within the scope of our interest – networking for economic advantage; or around shared purposes or ideals; or for personal and career development – it is quite possible that all these issues may apply to individuals who make up the network. Furthermore, these three broad categories apply equally both to individuals' motivation for joining a network initially and to the benefits they may realise as outcomes of their networking activity. The initial motivation for joining a network may change over time, as differing outcomes start to be realised. For example, someone might be sent to a regional development network by their firm to build collaborative relationships with competitors, but may find the network a source of excellent career development opportunities too.

Less obvious ties may link members of a network, and these may not be consciously understood by individual actors and may operate on a different level to the formal and overt reason for the existence of the network. These more complex motivations for forming strong network relationships may be voiced or unvoiced. Varying examples of the motivation for networking are found, for example, among business leaders in South Brittany (Box 1.1) and among young entrepreneurs in Turkey (Box 1.2).

BOX 1.1 TERRITORY AND SOLIDARITY IN THE BRITTANY REGION OF FRANCE

A case study of 25 small or medium enterprise (SME) business leaders in the Brittany region of France examined the social embeddedness of companies in their local region. In their responses, they tended to conflate their own actions with the value of the actions to their company, making little distinction between their business reasons for networking and a far wider social dimension which the researcher attributes to the notion of 'solidarity':

> the concept of solidarity [is] defined as a situation of dependence between people or between two or more organizations, but it can also be regarded as a social process facilitating collective action... Most of the time, solidarity requires a sense of belonging to a common entity such as a territory. In particular, this type of solidarity encourages the questioning of links that exist between local companies and their territory.

10 Networking: innovation and ideas

In the research that explored this idea of solidarity, the business leaders came up with a number of explanations of their motivations for networking. The most significant were:

- Sharing experiences
- Industry animation and events organisation
- Knowledge transfer
- Leaders' competencies development
- Business creation process
- Links with local government

The respondents described a mix of motivations, from straightforward business growth to a more complex identification with their local territory. The linkages to the territory often started in the names of the different networks, which were strongly tied to the town or the region. Thus the networks became places of encounter and interactions which utilised social relationships as a key mechanism in co-building a strong region with a buoyant economy. While this clearly made business sense, the SME leaders talked too about the value of giving back to the community and the importance of the region to their own sense of identity.

As one of them put it, 'We need to have roots in order to have wings' (adapted from Marinos, 2018).

BOX 1.2 SPIRITUALITY AND NETWORK COMMITMENT

The term 'Anatolian Tigers' is applied to groups of successful and outward-looking young entrepreneurial businesses in Turkey. In examining reasons for their success, researchers identified that members of these firms were highly likely to engage in local networking activity which added considerable value to their regional economies.

The common factor which built trust and commitment to shared networking activity proved to be a common spirituality. Here, the authors defined spirituality as:

> the effort to find one's ultimate purpose in life to develop a strong connection to co-workers and other people associated with work, and to have consistency (or alignment) between one's core beliefs and the values of their organization.

In their work, the authors argue that if spirituality is important in an organisation, as research indicates it is, then this definition applies even more at the level of the network, where shared spirituality is a common bond to bring unlike actors together. They demonstrate that as networks are entered into on a voluntary basis and have more scope to be driven and shaped by individuals, spirituality acts as a 'common bonding mechanism', which drives rather than follows trust and commitment.

Shared spiritual beliefs and values foster a sense of community and place. Shared spirituality, for these companies and their workers, is more important than the more obvious economic motivations for participating in the network such as winning resources or gaining business (adapted from Kurt et al., 2016).

It is possible too that emergent networking practices may change more rapidly in more informal economies (e.g. see an interesting case study from Ghana, reported by Darbi and Knott, 2016). They conclude:

> This study reveals the extent to which strategists may bring noneconomic and 'non-rational' personal and social considerations to bear on strategic decisions they make on behalf of the organisation. Full understanding of the strategy practices of informal businesses is unlikely without accounting for these kinds of influences.
>
> *(Darbi and Knott, 2016, p. 411)*

Thus, while our definition of networking lays emphasis on the intention of the network actor, it is important to remember that intention may be a shifting and somewhat opaque concept, not fully understood at an individual level, explained in different ways in different contexts and subject to change over time.

Boundaries to the definition

The definition above intentionally excludes networking activity, which results from relationships that were primarily entered into for social or leisure reasons. This is a deliberate decision on the part of the authors to set some boundaries around a subject that could otherwise be too broad to be discussed in a meaningful way.

There are some other forms of networks that are equally excluded from this present work. One of these is criminal networks. Organisations that exist for the primary purpose of criminal gain may fit our definition of improving business or services. However, the field of criminology is outside the scope of our concern here, not least because of the difficulty in building our empirical data through talking to those participating in such enterprises.

A second form of network that is not discussed here are large-scale and long-lived formal networks, for example, fraternal organisations such as Freemasonry. Clearly, networking within the scope of our definition happens in these kinds of societies. Nonetheless, the history, structure and rituals of Freemasonry are probably of more importance than the networking activity of the individuals in it at a given moment in time. Our premise for distinguishing between the

12 Networking: innovation and ideas

networks that interest us and such organisations as the fraternal ones we are excluding is a belief that, in the latter, sustaining the organisational structure into the long term is more important than supporting relationship building in the short term. In contrast, we will confine ourselves to formal networks whose mission is primarily focused on supporting business networking to a defined and boundaried end point.

In a similar way, permanent trade associations or professional bodies are also excluded. Again, we recognise that the process of networking is a significant outcome for these types of organisation. However, their primary purpose is likely to be different. They may be formed as lobbying bodies, or as training bodies or they may be required through legislation to act as regulatory bodies and to maintain the register of qualified individuals. Despite their importance, therefore, in the transmission of sector-relevant ideas and the support they offer for individual personal and professional development, we do not consider them to be primarily networks.

This leads to a further distinction to be drawn between networks and networking. Much of the formal academic literature which exists concentrates on the locus, the site, where networking occurs – the network. This is because it is relatively easier to study the organisation than the multiplicity of individuals who make up the network. It is not possible, nor is it desirable, to talk about one without the other. The nature of the network will shape and define the kinds of networking which happens within it. However, our primary purpose is to consider the process of networking. In this context, it is important to remember that while networks may have a formal intent and goal for networking, individuals within the network may find a more eclectic set of outcomes in terms of the benefits that they realise from participating. One of the great strengths of networking is the ways in which it allows for multiple outcomes from relationship building.

Is a network the same as a community of practice?

Here, we will distinguish between networks, teams and communities of practice (Lindkvist, 2005; Ashton, 2012). This is a more difficult distinction and it is perhaps better to suggest that these kinds of things exist on a continuum (as suggested by the editors of the *Journal of Management Studies* in their collection of papers reassessing this area; 'Limits to Communities of Practice', 2006). At one end of the continuum is the team – a semi-permanent entity which comes into being with a primary purpose of completing certain tasks or operations. This is thus clearly different from a network – an organisation whose primary purpose is to facilitate the building of relationships. However, in practice it may not be so clear-cut; many managed networks will have missions that include a number of operational outcomes.

Communities of practice are more difficult to define in relation to networking. The phrase came into being with the publication of *Situated Learning:*

Legitimate Peripheral Participation (Lave and Wenger, 1991) and related originally to a group of people who share a craft or profession, where knowledge and skills are held within the community and disseminated through membership of the group. This certainly seems like a networking process. The idea of a community of practice has since become extended to communities of interest – looser group- ings of people who share a common interest and who transmit knowledge and ideas from one to another, perhaps extending the theory beyond the point where it is helpful (Duguid, 2005).

Another extension of the initial theory around communities of practice can be seen in the idea of communities of inquiry, a particular form of activity which marries expertise with participatory democracy, with regard to matters of public policy (Shields, 2003):

> Common to all communities of inquiry is a focus on a problematic situation. The problematic situation is a catalyst that helps or causes the community to form and it provides a reason to undertake inquiry. Most problematic situations require further investigation and action (i.e., inquiry). Second, members of the community of inquiry bring a scientific attitude to the prob- lematic situation... In addition, the community is linked through participa- tory democracy. The parameters of the problematic situation and approaches to resolution are shaped by the interaction of the community and the facts.
>
> *(Shields, 2003, p. 511)*

Shields's conceptualisation of an idealised community of this kind is probably close to the kinds of networks which are discussed in Chapter 5. All these exten- sions of the core ideas derived from Lave and Wenger (1991) could be argued to be descriptions of networks, a term which is altogether looser.

Viewpoint 1.2 Networking in, and for, practice

I do facilitate a weekly drop in for black and minority ethnic participants of open courses that I've run over the years for black leaders, so that we have a kind of network to encourage each other, to share information about appoint- ments that are coming up, job opportunities, grant opportunities, funding opportunities, and to support each other to go for them.

Lindkvist (2005) distinguishes between communities of practice which may operate for extended periods (as with a team) and much shorter task-and-finish groups that come together for a limited time period to work collectively on com- plex tasks. Both these groups he sees as bound together through shared knowl- edge, but their epistemologies differ in a number of ways. His latter group, which he describes as 'knowledge collectives', have many of the same characteristics

14 Networking: innovation and ideas

that we attribute to networks. This can perhaps be summed up in the epistemological maxims which Lindkvist creates to distinguish between his two groups. Communities of practice, he suggests, say 'we know more than we can tell', an expression of their practices which reside in shared activity and shared narratives derived over a long period of working together. Much of that kind of knowledge remains unvoiced and unacknowledged, and therefore inaccessible to outsiders. His 'knowledge collectives' would say, 'we tell more than we can know', typifying the distributed learning of free agents with individual skills and multiple knowledge bases. This kind of knowledge is explicit, shared and debated, seeking to find and define the common ground between the competing ideas and understandings of the different players.

Viewpoint 1.3 Network learning as a 'knowledge collective'

Yeah, we all kind of had similar cultural backgrounds; but I tell you what we did have, anything we lacked in terms of diversity of skin colour or gender, we absolutely made up for in terms of cognitive diversity. We had a really, really, different range of skills, expertise, backgrounds and knowledge: and we pulled that together and synthesised it in a way that I've never done before, which was actually, it was tremendously exciting to be part of. So, you know, there's a lot of people would be very critical and very quick to criticise the formation of that team and how it came together and how it operated ....but, you know, for what we delivered and how we did it; I struggle to see how we would have accessed those skills and experiences through any formal mechanisms, cause it just doesn't exist.

This seems to us an excellent way of thinking about the epistemology of networks, laying emphasis as it does on the rapid dissemination of knowledge, and perhaps a cherry picking of salient information relevant to the issues of current interest for individual actors in the network. Similarly, Ranmuthugala et al. (2011), in seeking to evaluate communities of practice in healthcare, set their definitional terms so wide in their search criteria that they could certainly be viewed as having moved from discussing communities of practice to considering far broader knowledge communities, including those we would certainly describe as networks.

The emphasis in communities of practice theory on the social situation in which learning occurs is very important to the idea of effective networking. As we have argued above, networking is a purposeful activity – and learning is one of the principal reasons people engage in it. Working across organisational boundaries and supporting participation from community stakeholders (Shields, 2003) is also an important function for some networks, as we will explore further in Chapters Three and Four. Initially, our own research indicated respondents

FIGURE 1.1 Anticipated benefits of networking.

tended to connect their motivation for learning to reasons connected with their work or career identity, giving rise to our initial categorisation of learning as being a mix of personal development goals and economic ends, as set out in Figure 1.1. Later, as we discuss below, the model was refined to distinguish between outcomes largely focused on the individual and those deemed to benefit the organisation. This suggests that communities of practice theory closely relates to networking practice, as discussed by the individual respondents in our research.

Perhaps the difference between communities of practice and networks is most salient in relation to how distinctive is the workplace as the locus of learning. Where the community of practice is co-terminus with the workplace, this is not a network but a community of practice (although we discuss internal networking in Chapter 4). However, Lave and Wenger's extension of their idea certainly applies to networks with looser boundaries. Their view of learning is centred on the idea of a newcomer becoming part of a community by working in it, becoming engaged with it and moving towards a state of full participation in it. The individual learner will reconstruct aspects of their identity through becoming a member of the community of practice. Through the evolving relationships between the 'old hands' and the new members of the community of practice, learning happens; and it happens in large part because the newcomers are motivated to become full members of the community. The resonance of these ideas for networks is apparent. We therefore argue that networks are not exactly the same as communities of practice (as often the membership criteria are looser), but the two have much in common. In discussing networking, therefore, it is useful to look at the theories of learning derived from the idea of a community of practice.

Reciprocity and mutuality

At the heart of the definition we have developed for the purposes of this present work is the building of relationships. Relationships are a two-way process, and implicit in the definition is the concept of mutuality or reciprocity. The idea of networking carries with it the idea of benefit to all parties – everyone brings something to the table and everyone takes something away. It is therefore useful at this stage to have a brief consideration of the terms 'reciprocity' and 'mutuality' and to ask ourselves if these two are the same.

16 Networking: innovation and ideas

Reciprocity is defined as 'behaviour by which two people or groups of people give each other help and advantages' (Cambridge English Dictionary, 2021). In social psychology, it is seen as something which arises from social norms – one kind act begets another. In contrast, the term 'mutuality' has an association with the law, being embedded in contractual forms. This distinction is drawn by Pessers (2014, p. 151), who records:

> reciprocity as a social morality of duty, and mutuality as a contractual morality of rights.

Although formal networks may define the rights and responsibilities of members of the network, in practice these are hard to enforce. For our present purposes, it is therefore helpful to think of reciprocity as the key principle that underpins participation in a network – the network's members are bound through a social convention which emphasises the need to give back to others as well as to take benefits from membership in the network. This kind of reciprocity, sometimes acting against purely self-interested behaviour, is explored as a complex web of responses to the social signals of others:

> People repay gifts and take revenge even in interactions with complete strangers and even if it is costly for them and *yields neither present nor future material rewards.*
>
> *(Fehr and Gächter, 2000 p. 159, their emphasis).*

If this is the case even with trivial interactions with strangers, how much more so in a network? So it is not helpful to consider the ways in which networks operate as either based on rational economic principles or wholly altruistic. Rather, network relationships need to be seen as a shifting and dynamic set of sociocultural interactions based on both giving and receiving, but not necessarily equally or concurrently.

There are many reasons why individual members in a network may dissent from expected social norms in terms of networking participation and mutuality. So, while both reciprocity and mutuality may seem to be key ideas in networking, we have omitted both terms from our formal definition. Instead, we talk simply about 'building and managing relationships', mindful that this process can sometimes go unreciprocated, or at different times may feel unbalanced in terms of the contributions and the benefits experienced by a given network member.

Equally, too, it is important to remember that reciprocity, while important, is only one element of the social exchanges that happen in a network. In his seminal article on this, *The Strength of Weak Ties*, Granovetter (1973) reminds us that there is a number of different ways in which members of a network form ties to one another:

> the strength of a tie depends on …a combination of the amount of time, the emotional intensity, the intimacy (mutual confiding) and the reciprocal services which characterise the tie.
>
> *(Granovetter, 1973, p. 1360)*

Viewpoint 1.4 An international perspective on reciprocity

In Russia, and in other non-Western contexts, I think reciprocity is much more important, and the sense of obligation. If somebody's done something for you, then you – there's definitely a sense of obligation that you have to return the favour; and I think it's much stronger than in the West.

Outcomes of networking

Our definition above suggests there are three main reasons why networking happens:

1. To grow or improve businesses or services
2. To spread and promote ideas or ideals
3. To support personal and career development

Research indicates that these categories are fluid and that an individual may join a network with one idea in mind and gain benefits in ways not anticipated at the start. From our empirical research, we have expanded individuals' motivations for joining networks to six potential identified benefits they hope to achieve through networking. As we interviewed individual respondents, we found they reported that the actual benefits realised after a period of participation differed from the outcomes they anticipated as their initial motivation for becoming involved in networking activity, and that the experience tended to be richer than expected. Box 1.3 gives more information about this research and Figure 1.2 represents our findings visually.

BOX 1.3 OVERVIEW OF THE RESEARCH STUDY

Background research for this book was carried out throughout 2020 and in the early weeks of 2021. Following an initial pilot, an online survey link was disseminated via Twitter, LinkedIn and email lists to reach a convenience sample of people for whom networking was a relevant activity. The online survey included demographic questions and some basic questions about behaviour and attitude with regard to networking, finishing with an invitation to leave contact details should the respondent be willing to be contacted for further research.

The survey attracted 338 responses, 88% of which were from the UK.

Gender

	N	%
Man	116	34.6
Woman	215	64.2
Non-binary	1	0.3
Prefer not to say	3	0.9

18 Networking: innovation and ideas

Age

	n	%
18–21	4	1.2
22–29	55	16.3
30–39	83	24.6
40–49	70	20.7
50–59	73	21.6
60–66	45	13.3
67+	8	2.4

Employment

	n	%
Private sector	96	28.5
Public sector	164	48.7
Third sector (e.g. charity)	33	9.8
Other	44	13

From the population of the survey, 5% of those who had agreed to be approached for further work were then contacted and asked to participate in an in-depth, follow-up interview (which, because of the global pandemic, was carried out online). Ethical agreement was sought again at this stage and all interviewees were made aware of their ability to withdraw from the interview at any time. The profile for the in-depth interviews was as follows:

Gender

Male	*6*
Female	10

Age

30s	2
40s	2
50s	3
60s	9

Employment

Private sector	6
Public sector	4
Third sector	3
Other	3

Networking: innovation and ideas 19

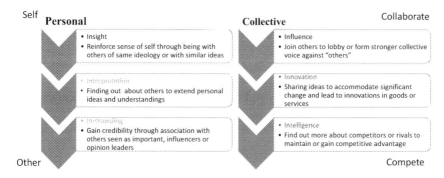

FIGURE 1.2 The network-IN model.

The six categories we identify are broad summaries of a range of outcomes from networking, representing a move from 'self' to 'other' at the level of the individual; and from 'collaboration' to 'competition' at a more collective level, recognising that individuals within networks may align themselves differently from their fellow participants; and that any given individual actor may change a personal perspective over time.

a. *In-crowding*: We use this term to cover all the outcomes suggested by respondents in terms of wanting to belong to an 'in-crowd' or a group considered to be opinion leaders or influencers within a given field or sector. The outcome sought by the individual concerned is to gain credibility or advantage through association with people seen as leaders or holding some kind of power valued by others.

Viewpoint 1.5 In-crowding

And there have been roles in the army, for example, when I was at X brigade where they pride themselves on finding wacky people who work in digital, and media and comms, and trying to harvest their civilian knowledge. But actually, they were really keen to almost squeeze me out like a sponge and work out who I knew and who I could influence.

b. *Intelligence*: Some join networks to find out more about their competitors or rivals, in order to ensure they stay abreast with significant or disruptive changes they are anticipating in their sector or field. Here, the outcome is to accrue competitive advantage for the firm or enterprise for which the individual works or is associated.

20 Networking: innovation and ideas

   c.   *Interpretation*: Others focus more on their personal learning, wishing to associate with others whom they consider are dealing with similar issues to themselves or, alternatively, to increase their understanding of individuals with different backgrounds who share a common purpose. The primary outcome sought here is an extension of personal ideas and understandings, helping to develop a deeper understanding of the world they inhabit. We heard many times of networks which formed among peers who started work together, and as careers advanced and diverged, the group maintained their links in order to gain a richer understanding from others in the same field but on different career paths.

   d.   *Innovation*: Some people will seek out networks with a membership from people with very different backgrounds to their own, with an explicit aim of sharing ideas that can lead to innovation in products or services, often at a time of significant change. These people may join such networks with a mandate from their employer or the interest group they represent.

   e.   *Influence*: For some people, the primary purpose of networking is to join forces with others in a similar position in order to develop a stronger collective voice with others outside the network, or to lobby for some kind of change to the mutual benefit of their fellow network members

   f.   *Insight:* The final outcome sought is to reinforce the ideas or ideals that an individual already holds for mutual support, or by mixing with like-minded others in order to strengthen and confirm their current world view. Through networking activity, the individual is helped to deepen, shape and better align beliefs, attitudes and behaviours. This is sometimes a defensive strategy for peers who share common pressures and who can thus support and maintain a collective sanity in an otherwise chaotic universe. In that way, networking can support a culture of resistance to an unacceptable dominant ideology.

Viewpoint 1.6 Insight

I also do like to stay in touch with what's going on, because I am still working. I still work with groups of people and it's good to connect people up actually.

Given the looseness with which the individuals we interviewed discussed their reasons for networking, and the overlapping outcomes which can potentially result from specific networking activity, it is helpful to examine each of these categories against some variables, identified in the literature, which confirm or extend our findings. These concepts will help to illustrate the context in which networking can potentially happen.

Networking: innovation and ideas **21**

i.   *Like/unlike*: While the membership of networks will vary and may not be controlled in any strict way, it is possible to distinguish between those which seek to recruit people from a similar background or those which wish to bring together people from unlike backgrounds. In the first case, collectively, this is likely to be for the purpose of increasing shared knowledge or synergy, or of speaking together with a common voice. In the second case, the purpose will be to facilitate the cross-fertilisation of knowledge or ideas across traditional barriers. In our model, at the level of an individual, we thus make a distinction between Insight and Interpretation. The degree of affinity between the members at any one time will then influence the likelihood, or otherwise, of more people joining with comparable affinity. Ramos et al. (2013) examined the emergence of what they describe as bottom-up business services networks in Portugal. They discuss 'homophily theory', which posits that network actors choose others similar to themselves to reduce conflict. Against that, they position 'heterophily mechanisms' based on the idea that opposites attract: coming down in the end to a suggestion that the most effective networks will have elements of both. Our research certainly confirms that individuals can happily join either type of network, distinguishing the outcomes they are seeking from each. Our model suggests this is a movement in networking activity from a focus on 'self' to a focus on 'other'; but the lived reality may also be that individuals will participate to different degrees in networks of people either like themselves or very different to themselves, in a fairly random way, depending on convenience and context as much as on any strategic approach to networking activity.

ii. *Reciprocity*: We discussed above that the notion of reciprocity is implicit in the idea of networks – they are based on relationships which are two-way processes. This does not necessarily mean that, at the level of the individual, everyone gets the same outcomes or benefits from participation at the same time. Some individuals may join a network specifically to gain benefit for themselves with no immediate intention of reciprocating. However, this attitude is likely to change over time, as it will not be sustainable in the longer term to have benefits flowing one way only. Thus, at any given time, an individual may vary in their commitment to the reciprocity principle. The benefits and harms of networking are discussed at greater length in Chapter 2.

iii. *Choice*: A third variable affecting participation in networking activity stems from whether an individual joins on a personal basis or as a representative of their organisation. For an interesting discussion on this, we recommend the analysis of 'contagion' as a metaphor for network learning through sociality and connectivity in inter-firm networks in the construction sector (Peters et al., 2016). At the most extreme, an individual may be required to participate in a network and have no choice over that decision. Thus, this variable may also influence motivation, at least initially.

22 Networking: innovation and ideas

iv. *Motivation*: This is thus another variable affecting the development of networking activity. It can be assumed that if they are networking on a personal basis, they wish to do so. In the case of an organisation, an individual may volunteer or be conscripted to become a network member. As we have observed, this latter category may impact on the extent to which the individual acts reciprocally, even where the intention of the network is for reciprocal outcomes. In turn, where an individual has a low personal stake in participating in a network, they may not actively seek for tangible outcomes from their membership.

v. *Outcomes*: Linked to choice and motivation is the clarity with which a network actor can articulate their primary purpose for participation, and the extent to which there may be congruence or dissonance between their avowed aim and the actual benefits realised.

vi. *Degrees of formality in network organisation*: Finally, there can be significant differences between the highly informal networks that individuals construct for themselves, some face to face and some online, in comparison with formal or managed networks which have structures and processes that exist independently of an individual, offering them a variety of opportunities in which they can choose to either participate or not.

Our discussion of some of the variables and choices around networking may imply a binary divide between some network characteristics, but we found this not generally to be the case. The reality is more complex, as some of these characteristics exist along a continuum. Equally, it needs to be reiterated that people's reasons for networking, and therefore the outcomes and benefits they gain from participation, will vary across their working lives. Some of our respondents were not able to identify outcomes they had explicitly gained through networking, but they still regarded it as an important part of their adult lives, both personally and professionally. The following Table 1.1 is thus a simplification of the complexity found in our data:

TABLE 1.1 Summary of factors impacting on networking benefits

Benefit	*Outcome*	*Affinity (like/unlike)*	*Reciprocity*	*Personal versus Organisational*	*Motivation*	*Formality*
Insight	Ideas	Either	High	Personal	High	Either
Influence	Growth	Like	High	Both	High	Formal
Interpretation	Career	Like	High	Personal	High	Informal
Innovation	Ideas	Either	High	Organisational	High	Formal
In-crowding	Career	Like	Low	Personal	High	Informal
Intelligence	Growth	Like	Variable	Organisational	Variable	Formal

Networks and technology

A notable omission from our adopted definition is the fact that we make no reference to technology, and the technological advances which have led to the point of our present time being defined as 'the network society' (Castells, 2004). This important idea is derived from the notion that the technological advances in the last 100 years have led us to a point where our primary social structure is the network, a series of interconnected communication nodes. This structure is in contra-distinction to what went before: hierarchies or bureaucracies based on organised power. While there is persuasive evidence of the massive impact of technological change on society, equally there is evidence the other way suggesting that though technology changes, humankind fundamentally remains the same and organises itself in recognisably similar ways.

Indeed, Castells cites Capra:

> the network is a pattern that is common to all life. Wherever we see life, we see networks.
>
> *(Capra, 2002, cited Castells, ed. 2004, p. 4)*

While this remains our own view that networking is a fundamental human activity arising from the social nature of humankind, we concur with Castells and colleagues in their view that technology has speeded up and changed the nature of networking. Our own research shows that digital networking has not replaced face-to-face networking; on the contrary, it has enhanced it and made it easier to sustain. Hampton (2004) reports that online networking forms only a relatively small part of most internet users' activities. Moreover, he goes on to say:

> Defining "virtual communities" as environments with clearly defined and discrete boundaries ignores the potential for social relationships on-line to be maintained off-line, and privileges the Internet as a separate social system. Social networks are cross-cutting and multi stranded. People use multiple methods of communication in maintaining their communities.
>
> *(Hampton, 2004, p. 220)*

For this reason, in our definition above we do not make specific reference to the methods used to support networking activity. Our assumption, based on our research, is that in the present age networks and network members will use all available channels of communication to support their network activities. We will explore aspects of this in later chapters, for example, the ethics of digital communications in Chapter 2 and geographical proximity or distance in Chapter 6.

24 Networking: innovation and ideas

Viewpoint 1.7 Face-to-face or digital?

I think it's essentially the same. I'm interested by people who say that they really miss face to face and can't get on with the technology, because I find that it's more immediate than the awkwardness of social interaction. Whenever you're networking, if you meet somebody for the first time, there's a slight social awkwardness. It's probably inherent in our makeup. In a way, somebody's either invading, or waiting to be invited into, your personal space. Whereas, if you have a Zoom call with somebody, they are immediately in your personal space. You've overcome that awkwardness because you've accepted the call. So that there isn't that little dance that you see in face-to-face networking. No matter how practised or welcoming people are, there's always that little sense of awkwardness at the beginning of a conversation.

It is problematic to reduce the impact on networks of technological advances to nothing more than the opening up new forms of digital communication. Such a viewpoint could certainly be criticised as under-playing the scale of globalisation through technologies which revolutionise financial markets, supply chains, the transmission of science and technology across state boundaries and the rapid spread of new ideas in ways that are both positive and negative.

> From the restructuring of business emerged the global, networked economy. From its success, and the simultaneous demise of statism, a new model of informational capitalism was constituted. From the opposition to its social, cultural and political consequences emerged new forms of social movement.
>
> *(Castells, 2004b, p. 22)*

These are all ideas we will look at further in subsequent chapters.

The problem with theories of networking

There is a key problem in any discussion of networks and networking which we will be addressing throughout this book. This relates in particular to the evidence base on which we are drawing for some of our detailed discussions (see Möller and Halinen, 2017, for a useful overview of the contested field of network management research from a business perspective). There is no shortage of theory relating to the topic of networks, and a wealth of interesting cases about networking in practice. The key problem is that there is almost no agreed common ground on any of the salient issues which arise, and not even a shared understanding of the concepts and parameters which need to be made explicit by commentators in this arena. Our purpose in writing this book is to extend our definition of networking as widely as possible, to offer insights and new understandings by synthesising knowledge gained from bringing together knowledge from differing fields and sources. This does lead to a number of problems which need to be made explicit at this point.

1. *Ethics*: There are a number of ethical issues that arise through an activity that is widespread but has not necessarily been the subject of specific ethical theorising. Networking tends to be considered as an activity that happens alongside other activities (e.g. managing customer relationships) rather than as a discrete activity in itself. This means that networking does not tend to feature in discussions on the ethics of business. This seems to us a significant gap in the literature and is thus the subject of our next chapter.
2. *Innovation and ideas*: The problem here is that innovation is a significant topic in its own right, as is well evidenced in the 2017 special edition of *Industrial Marketing Management*, which looked specifically at innovation and networking (Lindgreen and Di Benedetto, 2017). The literature on innovation often tends to be highly subject specific – looking at innovation and the work of innovation networks by the sector in which they operate, such as health or sustainability. This is problematic as economic sectors will be supported by empirical research underpinned by theory belonging to that specific sector, each field having different underlying concepts. It is neither possible nor desirable to attempt to reconcile these through some 'grand theory' of networking. Rather, we will see the diversity of the fields with an interest in networking and innovation as our opportunity to point out a direction for further in-depth reading. Finally, with regard to innovation, it is important to remember that networks may position themselves in varying places on the network innovation pipeline; some will be concerned more with developing and bringing new products to market, and others, like for example, the Health Innovation and Education Clusters discussed in Chapter 3, may have as their core mission speeding up the adoption and spread of innovation and ideas more widely.
3. *Specialist versus generalist*: A similar problem arises in relation to the membership of networks and the extent to which they are specialist or generalist. This relates to our point above: the affinity that an individual will seek to find in the people with whom they network or the extent to which they are like or unlike them. Highly specialist networks will operate in very different ways to networks whose purpose is to bring together as wide a population as possible. Because researchers tend to work in specialised fields, they therefore will (perhaps unconsciously) tend to examine specialist networks in their area of interest. This leaves more generalist networks less well examined, something we attempt to address further in Chapters 5 and 6.
4. *The social sciences*: There are interesting academic perspectives to be gained too from applying psychological or sociological insights to networking practice as well as economic ones (e.g. Granovetter, 1973; Darbi and Knott,

2016). However, against the interest of looking through different lenses at the same issues (Castells, 2004) is the problem that very different underpinning theory makes it challenging to derive a clear overview of the state of the field. Competing world views obscure a succinct overview of the salience of the findings from research interest in this topic over the last 25 years (Duguid, 2005).

5. *Methodological issues*: These also obscure the dissemination of research into networking. Single case studies, which attempt to investigate in some depth the experiences of individuals within the network, are criticised on the grounds they may not be generalisable. But attempts to produce a more systematic kind of theory are equally open to the critique that they oversimplify a complex and intricately embedded form of social activity.

6. *Effectiveness*: Finally, because of the complexity of reasons individuals have for networking, it can be hard to measure the effectiveness of the activity in any meaningful way. Many individuals network over their entire working lives, spending differing amounts of time doing so at differing points and moving freely between formal and informal networks as they become more or less available to them. At what point therefore does it become useful to evaluate the effectiveness of networking for that person? In a similar way, while it may seem easier to evaluate the effectiveness of a network rather than the process of networking, and for this reason most of the academic discussions of effectiveness relate to networks rather than networking, this is to some extent a false distinction. Any given network is made up of the individuals in it who are participating in networking activity; so to what extent can a network be deemed effective without drilling down to the experience of those participating and networking with in it?

Viewpoint 1.8 Why network?

Why do I bother? Because I have an interest in seeing what other people think. I do not want to be in an echo chamber all the time.

So, I may state that, if I look into my professional networks there are people who are thinking and feeling like me. That's the easy part, the emotionally supportive network. But then, there are also people who I respect very much on the professional level, who have very different processes to me in terms of their worldview, in terms of how they approach problems.

And that I find very interesting and enriching, maybe not so much on an emotional but very much on an intellectual level. So, this is the reason I make the effort to try to understand how they think. It's not an entirely altruistic process. I gain something from it. That's why I do it.

Conclusion

This chapter presents an overview of the purpose and key themes of the book, and includes an introduction to the work we carried out which led to our model of networking: the Network-IN model which categorises networking activity by the benefits that people aim to get from it. We use this model, together with ideas gained from the networking literature, as the loose organising structure for the book: by looking at both networking activity and networks from the perspectives of either the individuals or the organisations who are choosing to become involved. Our definition is the starting point for this – identifying three main aims for networking. The rest of the chapter extended the definition, discussed its boundaries and identified implications and issues that are to be explored further in later sections of the book.

Networking Narratives

1. Fem-Net-CA

The Fem-Net-CA was founded on the idea that... its tagline is something like...'we support you so you can support the world'. It's an organisation in California that was set up as a workspace with a difference. Their insight was, basically, there's a child care crisis, so they provided a place where you could have your child on site being cared for. Once you had a workspace; that interestingly, became quite a networking place, in the sense that they had a very strong community, so you feel like a member of a kind of club or workplace. And you experience the benefits of that. It's a smaller community of trusted, likeminded people.

It's all a lot of very smart women who just happened to be parents, professional women who care about furthering other women's development in the workforce. But because it wasn't set up as a professional networking development place, it's very much a kind of 'come as you are'. 'Come to feel seen and be seen', but in a kind of nurturing, holistic way rather than a kind of status driven way.

Since the start of the pandemic, when the physical space had to close, they use Slack as their social networking thing; and they have lots of different channels for various things. There's one for business growth books, that's important. I do loads of activism work for them, such as my anti-racism work, which led to working to combat voter suppression during the election. But there's also Slack channels called Potluck where people share recipes or a channel for parenting advice. They've done what they need to do to keep the doors open.

28 Networking: innovation and ideas

And that has changed the makeup of the membership some more, to be honest; democratised it so it's not so elitist, and I think that people respond to that well. So I'm saying there is a tension between the original founders who see themselves as the network leaders and the actual network taking on a life of its own, yeah.

So that's the closest thing I've found to an all-round holistic network; you know where you can be every facet of your personality there. So, the idea there is that I feel, that people feel, that they're getting so much out of the community, they want to give something back to it; so they will take charge of something.

They open a space every week and they have a topic. And you show up if you want to ask advice: or...or talk about something. They've done them on IVF fertility loss. They've done one on financial worries; they've done disordered eating. I get a lot of help with trying to return to work. There's a lot of women in my position who may be taking a break from the workforce and want to re-join; so, there's confidence building stuff there. I think it's quite a modern approach; recognised that balance across aspects of one's life is important, and so through this community, as it's grown; it's kind of grown as people need it to.

So, every day they have a community connection. For instance, at 10:00 am, you can log on and say hello to people: and everyone has a chance to, sort of, speak for a minute and it's just a social interaction, in these pandemic times. Now the membership's grown and I don't know so many members; there's this kind of body positivity do's and don'ts. I wouldn't.... I was pleased when I hit my, you know, weight loss goal after the babies, and in the 'old world' I would have celebrated it. Whereas now I didn't post about that, for fear of offending someone who had dysmorphia or something.

Ask yourself?

1. In terms of the benefits of networking identified in this chapter, what can you recognise in what the speaker is saying?
2. Do you agree with the speaker that Fem–Net–CA has quite a modern approach? What is distinctive about it?
3. Our definition talks about three main aims for networking, so how can a network like Fem–Net–CA support these?
4. Do you see any ethical problems or risks in their approach? What advice might you give to the speaker?
5. What features were inherent in the Fem–Net–CA model that helped them to adapt rapidly to the global pandemic?

References

Ashton, S.D. (2012) *From Teams to Communities of Practice*, Provo, Utah: Brigham Young University Scholars Archive

Cambridge English Dictionary (2021) 'Reciprocity'. Available at: https://dictionary.cambridge.org/dictionary/english/reciprocity (Accessed 10 March 2021).

Capra, F. (2002) *Hidden Connections: Integrating the Biological, Cognitive and Social Dimensions of Life into a Science of Sustainability*, New York: Random House.

Castells, M. (ed) (2004a) *The Network Society: A Cross-Cultural Perspective*, Cheltenham: Edward Elgar.

Castells, M. (2004b) 'Informationalism, Networks and the Network Society: A Theoretical Blueprint,' in Castells, M. (ed), *The Network Society: A Cross-Cultural Perspective*. Cheltenham: Edward Elgar, pp. 3–45.

Darbi, W.P.K. and Knott, P. (2016) 'Strategising Practices in an Informal Economy Setting: A Case of Strategic Networking,' *European Management Journal* 34: 400–413, http://dx.doi.org/10.1016/j.emj.2015.12.009

Duguid, P. (2005) '"The Art of Knowing": Social and Tacit Dimensions of Knowledge and the Limits of the Community of Practice,' *The Information Society* 21: 109–118, doi: 10.1080/01972240590925311

The Editors (2006) 'Point-Counterpoint: Limits to Communities of Practice,' *Journal of Management Studies* 43(3), 0022–2380

Fehr, E. and Gächter, S. (2000) 'Fairness and Retaliation: The Economics of Reciprocity,' *Journal of Economic Perspectives* 14(3): 159–181.

Granovetter, M.S. (1973) 'The Strength of Weak Ties,' *American Journal of Sociology* 78(6): 1360–1380, https://www.jstor.org/stable/2776392

Hampton, K. (2004) 'Networked Sociability, Online, Offline,' in Castells, M. (ed), *The Network Society: A Cross-Cultural Perspective*, Cheltenham: Edward Elgar, pp. 217–232

Kurt, Y., Yamin, M., Sinkovics, N. and Sinkovics, R.R. (2016) 'Spirituality as an Antecedent of Trust and Network Commitment: The Case of the Anatolian Tigers,' *European Management Journal* 34: 686–700, http://dx.doi.org/10.1016/j.emj.2016.06.011

Lave, J. and Wenger, E. (1991) *Situated Learning: Legitimate Peripheral Participation*, Cambridge: Cambridge University Press.

'Limits to Communities of Practice' (2006) *Journal of Management Studies* 43(3): 621–622, doi: 10.1111/j.1467–6486.2006.00604.x.

Lindgreen, A. and Di Benedetto, C.A. (2017) 'The Future of Industrial Marketing Management,' *Industrial Marketing Management* 67: 1–4, doi: 10.1016/j.indmarman.2017.09.009.

Lindkvist, L. (2005) 'Knowledge Communities and Knowledge Collectives: A Typology of Knowledge Work in Groups,' *Journal of Management Studies* 42(6), 0022–2380

Marinos, C. (2018) *Contribution of Business Networks to Local Solidarity*, unpublished working paper. University of Sud Bretagne.

Möller, K. and Halinen, A. (2017) 'Managing Business and Innovation Networks- From Strategic Nets to Business Fields and Ecosystems,' *Industrial Marketing Management* 67: 5–22, https://doi.org/10.1016/j.indmarman.2017.09.018

Peters, L. Pressey, A. and Johnston, W. (2016) 'Contagion and Learning in Business Networks,' *Industrial Marketing Management* 61: 43–54, http://dx.doi.org/10.1016/j.indmarman.2016.06.011

Pessers, D. (2014) 'The Normative Foundation of Legal Orders: A Balance between Reciprocity and Mutuality,' *Netherlands Journal of Legal Philosophy* 43(2): 150–157.

30 Networking: innovation and ideas

Ramos, C., Roseira, C., Brito, C., Henneberg, S. and Naudé, P. (2013) 'Business Service Networks and Their Process of Emergence: The Case of the Health Cluster Portugal,' *Industrial Marketing Management* 42: 950–968.

Ranmuthugala, G., Plumb, J.J., Cunningham, F.C., Georgiou, A.A., Westbrook, J. and Braithwaite, J. (2011) 'How and Why Are Communities of Practice Established in the Healthcare Sector? A Systematic Review of the Literature,' *BMC Health Services Research* 11: 273, http://www.biomedcentral.com/1472-6963/11/273

Shields, P. (2003) 'The Community of Inquiry: Classical Pragmatism and Public Administration,' *Administration and Society* 35(5): 510–538, doi: 10.1177/0095399703256160

Tamarit, I., Cuesta, J., Dunbar, R. and Sanchez, A. (2018) 'Cognitive Resource Allocation Determines the Organization of Personal Networks,' *Proceedings of the National Academy of Sciences of the USA* 115(33): 8316–8321, http://www.pnas.org/cgi/doi/10.1073/pnas.1719233115

Van Baalen, P., Bloemhof-Ruwaard, J. and Van Heck, E. (2005) 'Knowledge Sharing in an Emerging Network of Practice: The Role of a Knowledge Portal,' *European Management Journal* 23(3): 300–314, doi:10.1016/j.emj.2005.04.008

2

THE ETHICS OF NETWORKING

Introduction

Because networking is often informal and unstructured, it can escape the forms of scrutiny which bring checks and balances into business processes. This puts the onus on networkers to ensure the ethical probity of their actions. While networking, like any other form of human interaction and exchange, raises a number of ethical issues, the ethics of networking is a relatively underexplored area in the research literature. This chapter takes account of some key published studies as well as our own empirical research to discuss some of the dilemmas presented by networking, and point to their resolution in practice.

In particular, we examine:

*   Network as a form of friendship
*   Respect for self and others in networking, including respecting privacy
*   Inclusion and exclusion
*   Power and unconscious bias

We argue throughout that taking a consciously ethical approach to networking is more likely to produce sustainable mutual value than simply 'muddling through' without questioning assumptions that might otherwise be taken for granted.

Networking: good and otherwise

The practice of networking with its emphasis on reciprocal social interaction is, in many ways, an attractive alternative to more formal procedures for getting things done. Being able quickly to source information or to further a project through personal contacts appears, at least on the face of it, to be more natural

DOI: 10.4324/9781003026549-3

32 The ethics of networking

and efficient than resorting to impersonal bureaucratic systems. Creativity and learning are often associated with flexible, personal encounters rather than formal settings and routines. Furthermore, the informality of networking disrupts hierarchical structures in a potentially productive way. For example, a corporate event can throw senior managers together with junior colleagues who might never encounter them in the day-to-day organisational life, creating opportunities for influence and lobbying.

But this informal and unstructured aspect of networking creates potential ethical problems in practice. At their core is a lack of accountability for the processes and outcomes of informal networking beyond the norms of those involved; even then, the power to disapprove or to modify behaviour is unlikely to be evenly spread within the group. This is true of both individual and collective networking situations. For example, Dobos (2017) argues that personal networking as a form of career development can shade into corruption, as networkers curry emotional and social favour with decision-makers responsible for promotion or appointments. While such self-promotion can be risky to the networker by inviting extra scrutiny of their actual performance, it also subverts the principles of fairness and equal opportunities which should underpin selection processes.

> ## Viewpoint 2.1 Personal networking and career development
>
> I'm always quite careful about making sure that I can't be accused of any kind of nepotism or anything like that. I find actually, in my current context of the NHS, they're dreadful for that. There's almost an expectation that you've, em, greased the wheels before you go to an interview. It's just ridiculous. I don't mean this in a kind of corrupt way, but you're expected to, kind of, have spoken to all the members of an interview panel in a way which I wouldn't; you know, I just didn't.

At an organisational level, the social framework through which reciprocity operates can deteriorate into a system of mutual backscratching and cronyism, breeding injustice and inefficiency. Cronyism involves favouring certain people over others on the grounds of familiarity rather than merit when granting contracts or other opportunities. Begley et al. (2010) explain it, partly, as a defensive strategy in the absence of effective institutions to promote fairness, particularly in developing countries with collectivist cultures. But how does it differ from organised referral networks, such as the thousands of business clubs which meet regularly on a local basis all over the world? Some organisations may restrict membership to one representative of each relevant occupation to limit intergroup competition. So, for example, there may be just one tax accountant and one conveyancing solicitor who will recommend each other's services to clients based on their social relationship (Townsend, 2014, p. 145). It might be objected that this kind of reciprocity is not necessarily in a client's interest. On the one hand, the personal tie between network members whose professional fortunes depend on their reputations may create a layer of mutual accountability that operates in the client's interests. On the other hand, recommending a peer whose performance proved to be substandard would have an adverse effect on one's own credibility.

Viewpoint 2.2 Par for the course?

I had a conversation with somebody the other day about how everything was done on the golf course, and if you didn't play golf, that was it. You were excluded from any progression not just in that particular organisation, but in that sector, because they were all obsessed with golf. (Funeral directors I've heard are particularly golf orientated, which you'd never have imagined. Perhaps they have a lot of time on their hands during the day, I don't know?) But it's one of the things that people do; that does naturally exclude people

We are used to the concept of the fiduciary (or trusting) relationship between clients and professionals in areas like financial services (Audi, 2008). Without trust in the good faith and professional judgement of a broker, for example, the investment industry would be impossible to sustain, and investors and the wider economy would forego the potential benefits available. Codes of practice commit professionals to acting in the interest of their clients. But trust in a fiduciary relationship needs also to be justified by satisfactory performance and transparency (e.g. about terms of business). Extending these principles to networking, any recommended contact needs to be demonstrably competent, and the grounds of the recommendation need to be clear to the client in order to ensure ethical propriety.

Networking can help to raise ethical standards. Network members exchange influence, including moral influence and ideas, as well as information and resources. For example, an important driver for Health Innovation and Education Clusters in the UK, as discussed in Chapter 3, was the promotion of accountability as part of their mission to demonstrate the efficacy of investment in innovation. Chapter 5 covers the role of networking in facilitating positive social change (outlining some of the ethical complexities this presents and how they might be navigated effectively). There are many examples of networking generating sustained ethical critique of external social and political norms. The International Baby Food Action Network (IBFAN) forced Nestle and other manufacturers to clean up their infant formula marketing practices in the late 20th century. Since that time, it continues to hold manufacturers and other stakeholders accountable for departures from relevant codes (Rundall, 2021). The original movement has bred other networks in the 21st century campaigning against bottled water and dietary sugar (Muller, 2013).

34 The ethics of networking

These are, no doubt, worthy causes; but their existence does suggest a possible further ethical complication: that of mission drift within activist networks, perhaps fuelled by internal momentum in various directions. Does ethical expansion towards new causes by network members run the risk of leaving behind the original target group of concern? Or, to look at it another way, are networks pursuing social justice ever satiable, given the complexity and durability of the problems they seek to address? These questions are beyond the scope of the present chapter, but suggest future directions in networking research.

The following sections will discuss the more bounded ethical questions raised by our empirical research on networking, as practised in both personal and collective contexts. We will frame them with some key ethical concepts around friendship and our duties towards other human beings. Such duties include respect for individual autonomy and privacy, and may coincide with legal obligations whose neglect can incur serious sanctions. We will also touch on important issues raised by our respondents, such as authenticity in business behaviour and the exclusionary effects of networking on certain groups. While ethics is a relatively neglected area in research about networking, frequently voiced objections to the manipulative or insincere nature of networking relationships commend it as a subject of investigation and debate. As with any ethical topic, there are many different perspectives that can be defended. The important thing is to think through the wider implications of your networking activities, and be able to justify your position to yourself and other stakeholders in a consistent and sustainable way.

Networking as a form of friendship

Networking leverages personal relationships which are friendly in nature but lack the intensity and integrity of friendship for its own sake. Although professional relationships may lead to self-sustaining personal ties, the distinction between personal and professional friendships was made several times by our respondents.

The moral value of seeing friendship as an intrinsic good, which should not be tainted with ulterior motives, is upheld by Western philosophical tradition. Four centuries before the Christian era, Aristotle assigned friendship a fundamental importance in his vision of the good life: 'without friends no one would choose to live, though he had all other goods' (Nicomachean Ethics, VIII, i.). He categorises three types of friendship based on their purpose:

- Pleasure
- Utility
- Goodness

Friendship can be a source of pleasure, in that we enjoy certain people's company and find them amusing. Friendship can be a source of utility, as we seek and return favours and other benefits from friends. This sounds like the version most

The ethics of networking **35**

relevant to our discussion of networking. Finally, friendship can also have an altruistic, moral aspect as we look out for the good of the other person.

While acknowledging overlaps between them in practice, Aristotle prefers the third kind as the perfect friendship based on an unselfish but mutual concern for the other's good. Virtuous friends may be a pleasure to know, and may also do us good turns; but the friendship they represent is superior to the other kinds on two counts. The first is sustainability. Aristotle argues that pleasures fade alongside the friendships that provide them. Utility is similarly temporary. Our needs change over time, meaning that what we find useful one day may no longer be relevant another. Once the benefit ceases, so will the need for the friendship. Only the virtuous friendship lasts.

The second point of superiority is a moral one. Pleasure and utility can be enjoyed by both good and bad people as friends. But only good, unselfish people can participate in virtuous friendships. This point may seem circular, but it is important to Aristotle's view of how the good life is lived. Good people attract one another as friends. Good friends are an essential resource for the maintenance and development of virtue itself. Virtuous friendships make us better as friends and better as people.

Viewpoint 2.3 Crossing the line

He didn't change his behaviour and the kind of verbal, you know…still really went on. We're all, kind of, mates: drinking, eating lunch, eating dinner, socialising with clients. It does put you in the position where lines are crossed definitely and you don't say things that you ought. You find yourself saying: 'well I'd better not say "that's sexist"', or 'that's racist', em, because you're gonna lose the account if you mortify the client in front of everybody

As we have observed, business networking sounds like utility friendship, a view supported by Schonsheck (2000), who concludes in line with Aristotle that the dependence of such friendships on a flow of currently relevant benefits makes them ethically vulnerable. But as Drake and Schlachter (2008, pp. 856–857) argue with respect to supply chain relationships, utility-based relationships between suppliers and customers also demonstrate key characteristics of Aristotle's virtuous friendships because of their reciprocal nature. Virtuous friends, supply chain members and effective networkers must align themselves with one another's values and intentions, be committed to honest communication (in order to understand and satisfy such intentions) and be prepared to invest time establishing trust over the long term. Melé (2009) applies Aristotelian moral thinking on friendship directly to networking relationships and comes to much the same conclusion. While utility may be the dominant motivation, the capability of networking relationships to develop trust, co-operation and moral accountability

36 The ethics of networking

gives networking the potential to create social capital whose benefits (such as increased trust) extend beyond the immediate network to wider society.

One might object that Aristotle's ideal of virtuous friendship falsifies the complex mix of motivations and reciprocal benefits that underlies even the most high-minded friendships in the real world. As human beings, we may not even completely understand our own motivations for what we do. We can hardly claim virtue as our only guiding principle in friendship. Another potential problem with Aristotle is his argument that virtuous friendships are distinguished from less worthy versions by their permanence. Our relationships, like other aspects of human experience, are dynamic rather than static. So, it would be possible for a friendship originally founded on business interests to develop into a more authentic, personal bond which still has elements of business utility.

Thus, while both friendship and networking are open to abuse and short termism, it is possible to reconcile good practice in networking with an ideal of friendship which goes beyond that of mere utility, to overlap, at least in part, with the long-term, mutually beneficial ideal of friendship at the heart of Aristotle's idea of virtue. In practice, this makes considerable demands on the ethical networker (whether in an individual or organisational context) to be clear-sighted about their own values, selective about their relationships, explicit in their signalling, receptive, reliable and patient.

Viewpoint 2.4 But can I trust you?

When you have a network, especially if you have an inner circle and an outer circle in your network, you have to work on the basis of trust, but at the same time you have to work on the basis that nobody is to be trusted. So, there are some things that you wouldn't share unless you had a particularly long-standing relationship with somebody and knew that they would never abuse that or let that out. But I think it's a bit naive to share things with your network that really shouldn't be shared. You have to have that, little demon on your shoulder saying, 'Should I really be saying this?'

Respecting people as individuals

The expression 'working a room' (c.f. Kintish, 2014, p. 80; Townsend, 2014, p. 234), familiar in networking parlance, refers to a situation where the efficient networker systematically does the round of potential contacts at a networking event. It's not an entirely serious figure of speech, but it does imply that human beings are reducible almost to the level of items of furniture to be judged entirely on their utility. This problem of instrumentality, of seeing people as a means to an end rather than respecting them as autonomous ends in themselves, is a frequently voiced objection to networking. It has something in common with

The ethics of networking **37**

Aristotle's disapproval of the merely utilitarian friendship. However, at least utility-based friendship can accommodate reciprocity, whereas instrumentality tends towards one-sided benefit.

The classic philosophical case against instrumentality in this sense comes from Immanuel Kant (1724–1804), who distilled his moral philosophy in the 'categorical imperative' (so-called because it applies in all circumstances):

> I ought never to act except in such a way that I can also will that my maxim should become a universal law.
>
> *(Cottingham, 2008, p. 506)*

In other words, we should ensure that the principles (maxims) underlying our actions are generalisable. We should ask ourselves what would happen if everyone behaved in like fashion. The categorical imperative, as stated here, could be read as a version of the Golden Rule, 'do as you would be done by', so long as we bear in mind how important human freedom and rationality are to Kant's notion of 'doing' and 'being done by'. Kant uses the example of promises, a relevant one to networkers, to illustrate the relationship between individual maxim and universal law. If your maxim (principle of action) is that false promises are an acceptable way to get out of a fix of some sort, what would happen if it became a universal law? Of course, the whole institution of promising would collapse, as would the many social and economic benefits that stem from it.

But what really troubles Kant is that a maxim such as allowing lying in certain circumstances 'would be bound to annul itself' (Cottingham, 2008, p. 511). In other words, it would be exposed as self-contradictory and therefore irrational. Allowing lying in certain circumstances, extended to become a universal law, would open the door to widespread distrust of the veracity of any statement, and swiftly produce a 'post-truth' society where irrationality drives out reasoned discourse (we may even have got there already). Kant takes rationality to be essential to human nature and so to morality. Without it, we cannot exercise what he calls 'the goodwill', the ideal capacity to want good for ourselves and others, which forms the basis of right action. Kant's entire moral philosophy is based on the cultivation of the goodwill through ensuring our absolute freedom as rational beings to choose what we do. Otherwise, the idea of an individual's action being good or bad does not make sense, because there are so many situations where, in order to judge the goodness of an action, we would end up saying 'it depends on the circumstances'. Only by rising above any circumstances that might influence and limit our freedom to act and being clear-minded in our choices can we be sure to be doing good.

The interlaced nature of human activity means that we need to cultivate and facilitate this clear-minded rational freedom in others too. Rather like Aristotle's virtuous friend, we need to help others to do the right thing as part of doing the right thing ourselves. This is what Kant means when he enjoins us to:

38 The ethics of networking

> Act in such a way that you always treat humanity, whether in your own person or in the person of any other, never simply as a means, but always at the same time as an end.
>
> *(Cottingham, 2008, p. 512)*

Thinking of another human being simply as a means to an end, be it gaining information or resources in a networking context, reduces them to a tool, like a piece of furniture, rather than respecting their autonomy as a rational individual. Clearly, it would be wrong and profoundly disrespectful if a networker were to limit another's freedom by using deception or duress to extract a benefit. But Kant would go further and condemn any kind of interaction which falls short of respecting another human being's rationality and freedom, because it also damages their ability to act morally. At worst, networks that do not respect the autonomy and freedom of others risk becoming self-serving institutions of power, hierarchy and privilege, and through these abuses, will lead to self-contradiction and ultimately failure. Some examples of potential abuses are included in Box 2.1.

BOX 2.1 THE USE AND ABUSE OF POWER IN NETWORKS

Physical power: Power that operates along the lines of hierarchy through the use of superior force. While it is unlikely in a network that there will be physical coercion, there may be manifestations of psychological coercion or bullying.

Resource power: The control of resources, including the possibility of resources being used to give or withhold reward. In a network, these kinds of resources are likely to be non-physical such as status and influence.

Position power: This is the use of legal or legitimate power conferred through role or rank. The risk in a network which is informally put together is that the de facto decision-making power may not be bestowed or legitimised by network members. Some networks may operate through a self-selecting group which may be detached from the wider interests of members. In some cases, these may be the original founders.

Information power: It is often said that 'knowledge is power', but the risk in some networks is that information may be withheld or restricted inappropriately to serve the interests of some individuals. Alternatively, gossip or speculation may be shared under the guise of information or knowledge. Finally, confidential information may be elicited in an informal social setting, perhaps oiled by alcohol consumption, which may be by competitors, placing the source of the information at potential risk.

Expert power: Given the emphasis this present work places on the value of networking to spread ideas and innovations, experts and powerful people will be acknowledged in many networks. The abuse comes if the recognition of expertise is limited by factors other than genuine expertise, such as markers of esteem that are inequitably available. A second risk is that experts can be unsettled by new ideas which they view as unorthodox, and thus may stifle debate and potentially innovation.

Personal power: This rests with charismatic individuals, who may be a boon to a network with their personality, wit and charm. However, such power may be derived from success and can potentially sour if the star finds himself or herself eclipsed by newcomers.

Negative power: This is the power to challenge or to block, which is sometimes useful and important in keeping the networking thriving. It becomes problematic when used inappropriately to support personal or organisational interests, or to exclude others (adapted from Handy, 1993).

Notoriously, moral freedom for Kant includes freedom from emotional rewards for good behaviour. He would, for example, see doing someone a favour because it made you feel good as morally inferior to doing someone a favour simply because they needed it. Motives of self-interest, empathy and even affection, which we might expect to feature in networking relationships, are morally suspect in this analysis, as they too interfere with our complete rational freedom to do the right thing.

You may well be thinking that this is an absurdly high-minded and impractical approach to moral reasoning about networking behaviour. Kant's uncompromisingly rational prescription for moral behaviour appears to ignore the emotional side of being human and to deny the moral worth of any motivation except stern duty. But his basic principle of respect for persons is difficult to argue with. If, as suggested earlier in the chapter, you think through your approach to networking in order to justify it to yourself and others, Kant's radically idealistic analysis can be a helpful framework. Several of our interviewees, for example, expressed something close to disgust at what they saw as attempts to suborn them through the instrumental bonhomie they associated with networking in practice. Kant would agree, seeing this as an undignified departure from how relationships should stem from the disinterested goodwill he takes as the yardstick of moral action. Note too that he includes 'your own person' in his categorisation of humanity to be respected as an end in itself (Cottingham, 2008, p. 512). Some interviewees reported their reluctance to be anything other than themselves as a reason for avoiding networking and the insincere friendship that it might require of them. In this sense, they were insisting on their own persons as free to act as authentic, autonomous moral selves in just the way that Kant indicates.

40 The ethics of networking

> ## Viewpoint 2.5 Why am I doing this?
>
> Authenticity is a huge kind of value for society; and I think lots of social media, in whatever form that is, takes people away from authenticity. And I think it's also kind of bullying because I think, in the end, that the kind of companies that engage in mad marketing, you know, 'networking', tell their employees that they have to be a certain kind of person and that anybody that isn't that isn't, you know, is somehow flawed. And you have to be inauthentic to fit into that pattern.
>
> Now I don't know whether agencies nowadays really are like that. I think there are agencies that have very genuine cultures and they pick people, and they really believe in what they're doing, but I think it can veer into that territory. And if you're desperate not to lose an account, em, I think it, ...it can lead you where you're building those phoney friendships.

So, while Kant's moral requirements appear to be impossibly exacting, they tally with the reservations many express about networking in practice. They also suggest an approach to networking that goes beyond the principle of reciprocity (important as that is in networking) to 'pay it forward' in the popular phrase (Hyde, 1999).

Building social capital, offline or online, depends on being prepared to take steps from which there may be little prospect of immediate personal benefit, such as doing favours with no obvious return or being nice to strangers on social media. Part of the motivation for such altruism is the conviction that, over time, the cumulative effect will advantage everyone. Hence the emphasis on patience in building and managing network relationships, discussed in Chapter 4. This can be seen as complementary to Kant's imperative to treat others as ends in themselves, encouraging them through kindness rather than demanding short-term returns which might actually limit the eventual value available from a relationship. Throughout the present work, we emphasise the reciprocal nature of networking – that everyone brings something to the table and everyone takes something away. It is important to understand that in the most effective networks, this is unlikely to be a 'tit-for-tat' return. Rather, through sharing knowledge, exploring ideas and supporting others, the individual will themselves gain new insights and benefits possibly beyond their immediate short-term expectations.

Privacy

Kant's ideal of treating humanity as an end, not just as a means, points towards networking which respects the other person and oneself as an individual. As well as respecting the autonomy of individuals, this includes respecting their

The ethics of networking **41**

privacy. Getting to know someone involves getting to know about them, and thus acquiring, storing and possibly sharing a considerable amount of personal information. With the exponential growth of computing power and storage capacity over recent decades, the term 'personal data' has taken on a very specific meaning.

For the purposes of the 2016 General Data Protection Regulation, which governs information rights in Europe but has parallels with legislation elsewhere, it covers any information which can be linked to a living person and/or used to identify them (ICO., n.d.). Processing such information (which includes gathering, storing, combining or sharing it) can only be done with the express knowledge and consent of the individual concerned. At one time this would have been a case of good manners, but now it is a matter of law in many countries; so networkers need to be aware of the principles involved and ensure they act not only ethically but also legally.

Organisations have a duty to make employees aware of the rules governing the use and storage of personal data. While personal or household activities may be exempt under the law, such an exemption only applies where there is no connection to a professional or commercial activity. The informal and often unboundaried nature of networking may lead into grey areas about the relevance of the legislation to personal networking activity. Individuals networking on their own account are therefore responsible for understanding and incorporating the principles of good data protection (Box 2.2). Doing so helps nurture the trust which results from competence and transparency, as discussed earlier in this chapter.

BOX 2.2 OVERVIEW OF PRIVACY GENERAL PRINCIPLES

A detailed account of data protection rules is beyond the scope of this book. There are plenty of resources available online which provide authoritative guidance in line with local legislation. The following general observations aim at underlining the link between data protection principles and ethical conduct.

According to the UK's Information Commissioner's Office (ICO, n.d.), the seven data protection principles are:

- Lawfulness, fairness and transparency
- Purpose limitation
- Data minimisation
- Accuracy
- Storage limitation
- Integrity and confidentiality (security)
- Accountability

42 The ethics of networking

These principles respond to the rights of the data subject (the individual to whom the data refers). Such rights (based on a Kantian respect for the individual) include being able to access one's personal data as held by others and have it deleted, corrected or restricted. Working down the list of principles, the implications are that data on networking contacts should be gathered with their knowledge and consent and used only for the purposes intended by them. Emails, addresses, telephone numbers and other identifying details make people vulnerable to unsolicited approaches (and potential harms) from which they have every right to be free.

It helps, therefore, to have a minimal approach to how much information you collect and store. Be guided by the limited and agreed purpose of such data at the time of collection rather than amassing details because they might come in handy one day. Data, like the people to whom they refer, age. It therefore makes sense to review and check contact details on a periodic basis to ensure their accuracy, and whether the contacts concerned are still relevant to your networking intentions (and vice versa). Given the long-term nature of many networking relationships, this is something that needs to be scheduled as a regular part of any networker's routine. It has the practical advantage of providing an opportunity to get in touch with people with whom you have not had contact for a while and demonstrate your transparency and responsibility when so doing. Deleting data that are no longer relevant or useful is a good way to implement the prioritisation that supports effective networking. It need hardly be said that an essential part of data protection is to ensure that data are stored in such a way that they cannot be accessed by anyone who does not have consent to do so.

The value of networking often consists in bringing together people you know but who don't know each other; so you need to find ways of making links without sharing personal data in ways that have not been authorised by the people concerned. Being conscious of how you are implementing each of these principles on a day-to-day basis will allow you to be accountable, both ethically and legally, for the information which is, in many ways, the key resource underlying your ability to create reciprocal value through networking. The ethical principles which should underpin your behaviours here relate to transparency over confidentiality and consent.

Data subjects have a responsibility to protect their own privacy as well as that of their contacts (remembering Kant's encouragement to respect our own persons as well as other people). This is particularly the case in online networking, where you make the decision to share information about yourself on the web. Many networkers make an absolute distinction between their personas on different sites, reserving LinkedIn exclusively for professional concerns. Whatever platforms you choose and for whatever purpose, it makes sense to become completely familiar with the privacy settings available to you in filtering access to different parts of the information you share with your chosen groups.

Viewpoint 2.6 Social media as a social issue

There are huge issues around the kind of social forms of networking that we're going to confront as a society, aren't there? Like, are the online platforms going to be regulated? Coz they say: 'I can't possibly edit all of that'; 'I can't, em, sieve it enough, cos I haven't got the resource yet'. They've gained their profits through allowing those sheer numbers of people onto their platforms; and, if they weren't a digital platform, if they were some other kind of, you know, hard medium like a magazine, or a newspaper or a book they would be subject to much more rigorous demands. But that is their responsibility: so, I think the ethics of most of the platforms that allow social media is going to become a social issue.

Inclusion and exclusion

By their very nature, networks include some people and exclude others. Exclusion may be a matter of injustice to those excluded by depriving them of benefits, possibly because of the complacency or prejudice of existing network members. As remarked at the beginning of this chapter, the informal nature of networking means there may be little accountability for processes or outcomes, and this is extended to unjustifiable exclusion. The research of economists Currarini and Mengel (2016) suggests a default setting of homophily (attraction to similar others) and in-group bias (preference for those like oneself) in network formation. This merits resistance on both practical and moral grounds. A lack of diversity may limit the range of information and new thinking available to network members. It may also lead to a defensive mindset resistant to external scrutiny or criticism, an example of groupthink (Janis, 1982) with demonstrably adverse consequences.

Viewpoint 2.7 How broad are my networks?

People tend to go with 'people like us', or whatever the phrase is. And that is why, when you asked me about the networks I was in, I feel they are very varied. I suspect they are probably not. Because I have a bias for networks with people that are like me, I might assume that they are probably varied; but I suspect that under certain criteria they won't be. So, when I'm aware of opportunities that might arise with people, that's why I try to widen the opportunities to people who might not have come across them because of that very reason. If you only choose the people that you know or ask the people that you know, you end up with a very narrow pool of diversity, be that ethnically or cognitively or whatever.

44 The ethics of networking

Excluding others for no good reason is not necessarily a deliberate process. Unconscious bias, the unacknowledged assumptions and stereotypes we carry in our heads about other people, is a powerful influence on our choice of associates. Bohnet (2016) cites a Harvard Business School case study exercise (developed initially by McGinn and Tempest, 2010), in which students were asked to evaluate a Silicon Valley entrepreneur called Howard as a potential networking contact. The same case study, with the protagonist rechristened Heidi, resulted in much lower evaluations – even from broadly identical groups of students. What passes for entrepreneurship and confidence in a man was dismissed as pushiness and arrogance in a woman because of unconscious bias.

Viewpoint 2.8 Affirmative action programmes?

Well, certainly, if it gets people access to opportunities, I think they're a good thing. We've had positive discrimination for a very long time. It's just that it's been in favour of white men.

But often, there is little that is unconscious about exclusivity. Our own research revealed 'in-crowding' (the desire to be part of a group perceived to be influential and credible within a particular field) as a motivation for networking. There is thus a psychological incentive for such groups to be selective about whom they admit lest their claim to authority be diluted. The question to be considered here is who makes the decision on who is included and who is excluded, how open are these decisions and can they be challenged? As well as the potential harms that may result for the excluded, the benefits of new learning and wider insights will also be lost to the 'in-crowd', perhaps without anyone realising. Thus, the social capital of all is reduced.

Viewpoint 2.9 Learning from difference

I was working with somebody who I'd been at Sandhurst with who I could not stand at Sandhurst. We really despised each other. And the pronoun they use is 'they'; they are very specific about you getting that right. And if you get that wrong, stand by to get told off. And on lots of different levels, on almost any contentious political issue, they have got a very strong opinion. So that can go one of two ways with somebody like me, because I can be quite forthright and blunt. It can either be incredibly interesting, we can have a really interesting conversation and it can stretch my horizons; or the other risk is, I shut that down.

And actually, I pushed myself quite hard to really go with it and work with that individual and understand their context; or try to understand their context. I suppose. And that relationship absolutely blossomed and I realised how narrow-minded I'd been in the past.

The ethics of networking **45**

There can also be economic reasons for keeping networks relatively impermeable. For example, the Chinese system of *guanxi* can be interpreted as a traditional form of relationship marketing drawing on sophisticated cultural and ethical commitments which Western aspirants to market entry need to respect, understand and comply with (Wong and Chan, 1999). Alternatively, *guanxi* can be seen as more akin to a self-serving stranglehold on economic power by incumbents at the expense of innovators, leading to corruption, inequity, societal harm and the triumph of elites over attempts at regulation (Li et al., 2019, p. 665).

Viewpoint 2.10 Pushing back on power

My personal observation is not in the Western context, but more in my Chinese family's context. I think there's some kind of power issues, power imbalances there. The word 'abuse' is probably too strong, but sometimes people may tend to use their power and try to persuade people in their network to do something for their purposes, that actually may do harm to other people. As far as I know, my mother comes across someone like that in the circle of the business that she does. But she consulted her brother and other people around her who gave her the answer: 'don't do that!'

This suggests a more critical interpretation of networking in general as the exercise of power by the powerful to protect their interests. Gender is a case in point, with 'old boys' networks all too literally acting as barriers to progression for women in organisations (cf. Durbin, 2011). Socratous (2017) notes the exclusion of women from male-dominated professional and academic networks in Cypriot society. She explains this partly on cultural grounds, referring to the legacy of traditional gender roles in a rapidly modernising society, and partly on the grounds of choice by women themselves who, she argues, avoid networking activities which would make them uncomfortable. The networking activities in question, many of them involving watching or playing sport, are chosen by men and are by nature male dominated. The effect is to deprive women of informal contacts and opportunities to advance their careers on a par with their male peers. In a similar way, others may be excluded on grounds perhaps of race, of sexual orientation, or just that unvoiced and discriminatory sense that 'their face doesn't fit'.

Because of the importance of heterophily (a tolerance of those different from oneself) in exposing network members to a wider range of ideas and information than they would ordinarily encounter, exclusionary networks might be expected to contain the seeds of their own destruction. While waiting for this to happen, the excluded can and do form alternative groupings where they can resist and subvert the hegemony which seeks to keep them in their place. Alsop (2015) points to the example of work-based book groups as a resource for professional networking by women. Such forums enable instrumental networking

46 The ethics of networking

(the exchange of job-related information and opportunities) but also expressive networking (a no less real but more social form of mutual support). Engaging in literary discussion meant members frequently related fictional situations to both personal and professional experience. While the majority of the book groups studied was open to all sexes, members appreciated the alternative they offered to the masculinised norm of socialising around drinking or sports.

Implications for practice

This chapter began by drawing attention to the positive and negative moral consequences that networking can have – from subverting recruitment processes to pressuring multinational companies to act more responsibly. Your view of the rights and wrongs of these examples will depend on your own value perspective. For example, you may feel that recruitment processes leave a lot to be desired in terms of fairness and we should reward the initiative and commitment shown by candidates who network to get themselves noticed. Or you might feel that multinational companies, on balance, do more good than harm because of their role in economic development and perhaps present too easy a target for single-issue campaigners. Your view of the rights and wrongs of networking of any sort will depend on your personal ethical analysis of the situation. It therefore pays to step back from time to time to revisit your assumptions and principles to ensure you are comfortable with how your networking activity looks to yourself and others. Part of effective networking is having a clear sense of what you can offer your contacts. This includes your values as much as your skills and other resources.

Part of this regular reflection can usefully address what is being exchanged and why in your networking relationships. We will have more to say about the nature of exchange in Chapter 4, but Aristotle's categorisation of different kinds of friendship suggests being conscious of the extent to which a relationship is based on utility – literally, using other people. Becoming more aware of your own motivations for networking can help in avoiding insincerity and exploitation, while still leaving room for a relationship to become something more perfect in the Aristotelian sense of friendship. As we have seen above, an Aristotelian framework for personal networking will emphasise:

- Being clear-sighted about your own motivations and the benefits you hope to realise from your networking activities
- Being selective about who you associate with, ensuring that those with whom you form longer-term networking relationships share your values
- Being explicit with others about your values, motivations and anticipated benefit realisations
- Being receptive to the belief systems, autonomy and privacy needs of others
- Being reliable in your commitment to reciprocity
- Being patient in your expectations of networking benefit

The ethics of networking **47**

Kant's uncompromising prescriptions for human behaviour appear difficult to draw on for practical purposes. However, his emphasis on respect for the human person provides a sound basis for networking. Rather than seeing one another as merely the means to securing benefits such as information or resources, networkers have a mutual responsibility to recognise themselves and others as ends in themselves. A first step to operationalising this principle might be to be more explicit about the nature of the networking relationship. This can potentially be clarified through ground rules, or an informal but overt contract. When joining a managed network, you can ask if there is an agreed Code of Conduct for network members, and if not, suggest at the right time that such a document would be useful to help everyone navigate their relationships.

Viewpoint 2.11 Being explicit

All the time, and from the outset, ground rules for working. Power is very much a part of that. So, before we have ground rules, I ask participants to identify the power relationships that might have an impact on individuals' ability to fully participate; or to be heard and taken seriously.

A second step in line with Kant's principles of respect for the human person might be to consider the opportunities for personal development that networking presents. Can you help someone become a more independent thinker through a networking relationship, corresponding to Kant's encouragement to exercise and develop human rationality and freedom? And in the same vein, can your networking relationships help you to develop your own autonomy as a moral agent? Practical examples of this might include:

- Acting as a mentor or entering into a peer mentoring relationship
- Sharing knowledge through passing on useful links or journal articles
- Discussing more complex professional dilemmas
- Supporting others in times of difficulty
- Calling out behaviour you find inappropriate or helping people to understand the impact of their choice of language on others

Viewpoint 2.12 Building trust

Repeated interaction with somebody builds trust. On the one hand, there's the initial elements of similarity that could potentially create a grounding for developing trust. But then it needs to be fuelled by repeated interaction and keeping promises and commitments or not.

48 The ethics of networking

TABLE 2.1 Developing a personal ethic for networking

Everyday professional framework (e.g. 4 Ps)	Ethical issues	Examples in practice
Product	My manifested network practice: • Transparent • Selective • Trustworthy • Competent • Benevolent	• Am I explicit about my networking behaviours, for example, ground rules or contract? • Do I disassociate myself from those who behave inappropriately? • Am I reliable? • Does my networking benefit others as well as myself?
Place	The ways in which my network is made available: • Inclusion • Patience	• Do I meet people in accessible places, for example, meeting in a pub may be an issue for non-drinkers? • Time – may be difficult for parents or carers
Price	The cost to self and others of being in my network: • Generosity • Flexibility • Equity	• Do I freely make available my time and knowledge? • Do I share things equally with all or do I privilege some over others? • Does participation in my network cost some people more than others?
Promotion	How I communicate within the network: • Discretion • Open-minded	• Do I respect the privacy of others? • Do I ask permission to share their personal information? • Do I maintain confidentiality? • Do I close down legitimate ideas that are different to mine? • Am I prepared to listen?

We began this list of practical implications with encouragement to networkers to develop a greater consciousness of their values and ethical assumptions to be able to account for their networking. Self-awareness is also the key to reducing the bias, both conscious and unconscious, which contributes to inequitable exclusion in networking. According to Eurich (2017), 95% of people think they are self-aware, but the reality is nearer 10%–15% (her research required knowledgeable others to confirm respondents' self-ratings). Techniques to increase your

The ethics of networking **49**

understanding of your behaviour and motivations, and what these might mean for other people, include asking others for feedback and introspective activities such as keeping a reflective journal. The SOC-ACT checklist, featured in Table 5.1 of Chapter 5, is a useful tool to structure reflection and has the advantage of being specifically designed to help network volunteers manage ethical sensitivities. Conceived to support networking in the context of social change, it is readily adaptable to any networking situation to help reveal and navigate ethical issues.

With regard to the specific ethical ideas discussed above, we recall Kant's 'categorical imperative' that the principles you adopt should be generalisable beyond the context in which you espouse them. A practical implication of this is that your networking behaviours should accord with any other framework you use to manage and regulate your everyday conduct. These could include organisational Codes of Conduct, professional regulatory standards or religious beliefs. It could even include business models that you use to analyse and optimise your work activities. We suggest one way of looking at this as an example in Table 2.1, using the well-known 'Four Ps' marketing mix as the everyday framework. Our suggestion here is that you can adapt any framework that you know well to help you become more self-aware about your networking practices. These practices should be consistent with the expectations you have of yourself elsewhere in your personal and professional life.

Conclusion

In spite of its relative neglect in research on networking, ethics is an important aspect of sustainable and effective networking practice. Networking produces moral consequences, both positive and negative. But it also has ethical force as a process in itself. Because of the importance of friendly relationships in networking, participants risk insincerity and exploitation, unless they are clear-sighted about their intentions and the basis of their interactions. To a large extent, the reciprocity that sustains voluntary exchange relationships protects participants' interests over the long term. If a partner feels that there is insufficient mutual value, a relationship will not last. But networks benefit from members going further than mere reciprocity to exercise generosity towards other members where the opportunity arises. This avoids instrumentality in relationships and increases social capital. Cultivating an attitude of respect underpins this developmental approach to networking.

Networks, while porous, still have the power to exclude. This disadvantages the excluded group as well as depriving the network of what they have to offer (which may be considerable, especially if they introduce more diversity). In this and other ways, a consciously reflective approach to networking can produce practical as well as ethical benefits.

50 The ethics of networking

Networking narratives

2. Being excluded

In my last firm there was a group of partners who were Oxbridge and who made it their business as a group to go every year to a rugby match; to the Oxford and Cambridge rugby match at Twickenham. They never invited me: never! I would have liked the recognition that I was their equal.

It did reinforce a sense of exclusion. I mean, of these guys there were three of them in London, one in Leeds; so, there are four guys. Now there was no other female in the firm who was Oxbridge. I could not set up an equivalent social opportunity if I'd wanted to. It was a reflection of where I stood in the firm.

Let me tell you another story about exclusion from my own experience. Actually, if you can publish this, it would be great! (laughs).

My department where I worked dealt with one main client, and that client, every year, had an annual dinner. I was at this firm, working for this major client, for 27 years and for at least 17 of these years and probably more; no, I think about 25 of those years, I was a partner. Not once was I, ever, invited to this annual dinner with our clients; not once, but I was aware that others who are my equals were invited.

So, the problem was that I raised it with my partners as to why am I not invited; and I got evasive replies and eventually somebody came specially from London to Leeds to talk to me about why I wasn't invited. Essentially, the message was 'we don't know, but these invitations are not ours to give, can't help you'. That was the attitude: don't know, can't help you.

I was actually lied to because at one point I was told: 'Oh well the reason is...'. It was suggested to me then that the reason I wasn't invited was because I wasn't a sufficiently senior partner. The other people who were going were more senior; that was what was implied. But I managed to discover that a more junior partner than me was going. So, when I put it to them that this wasn't true, they were a bit caught out and that's when the partner in question said, 'right, I'll come to Leeds to explain why you're not invited'. Which he duly did; he took the train, came all the way to Leeds to tell me essentially that he didn't know.

It should be inclusive shouldn't it? And it didn't make any sense that there I was, a partner: I was considered good enough to be a partner but not...for some reason, they didn't want to present me as part of their team. It didn't make any sense. It was very hurtful. And, yes, it was definitely a mechanism there to make me feel bad.

Ask yourself?

1. You are advising the male partners before they visit Leeds – what arguments could you advance to persuade them to change their behaviours? How would you counter the answers you anticipate they might give?
2. Imagine you are advising the female speaker – what options are available to her to change the situation?
3. The ethical frameworks considered in this chapter are largely derived from Aristotle and Kant – what light do their teachings cast on this situation?
4. All the players in this scenario are lawyers – how do you advise they develop a Code of Conduct to regulate their informal professional networking? What things would you include in the Code?

References

Alsop, R. (2015) 'A Novel Alternative. Book Groups, Women, and Workplace Networking,' *Women's Studies International Forum* 52: 30–38, doi: 10.1016/j.wsif.2015.07.006

Audi, R. (2008) 'Some Dimensions of Trust in Business Practices: From Financial and Product Representation to Licensure and Voting,' *Journal of Business Ethics* 80(1): 97–102, doi: 10.1007/s10551-007-9435-z

Begley, T.M., Khatri, N. and Tsuang, E.W.K. (2010) 'Networks and Cronyism: A Social Exchange Analysis,' *Asia Pacific Journal of Management* 27: 281–297, doi: 10.1007/s10490-009-9137-4

Bohnet, I. (2016) *What Works: Gender Equality by Design*, Cambridge, MA: Belknap Press of Harvard University Press.

Cottingham, J. (ed.) (2008) *Western Philosophy: An Anthology*, 2nd ed., Oxford: Blackwell Publishing.

Currarini, S. and Mengel, F. (2016) 'Identity, Homophily and In-Group Bias,' *European Economic Review* 90: 40–55, https://doi.org/10.1016/j.euroecorev.2016.02.015

Dobos, N. (2017) "Networking, Corruption, and Subversion" *Journal of Business Ethics*, 144(3), 467–478. doi: 10.1007/s10551-015-2853-4

Drake, M.J. and Schlachter, J.T. (2008) 'A Virtue-Ethics Analysis of Supply Chain Collaboration,' *Journal of Business Ethics* 82(4): 851–864, doi: 10.1007/s10551-007-9597-8

Durbin, S. (2011) 'Creating Knowledge through Networks: A Gender Perspective,' *Gender, Work and Organisation* 18(1): 90–112, https://doi.org/10.1111/j.1468-0432.2010.00536.x

Eurich, T. (2017) 'Increase Your Self-Awareness with One Simple Fix,' *TEDxMileHigh*, November [Online]. Available at: https://www.ted.com/talks/tasha_eurich_increase_your_self_awareness_with_one_simple_fix (Accessed 6th March 2021).

Handy, C. (1993) *Understanding Organizations*, 4th ed., Harmondsworth: Penguin.

Hyde, C.R. (1999) *Pay It Forward*, New York: Simon and Schuster.

ICO. (n.d.) 'General Data Protection Regulation,' [Online]. Available at: https://ico.org.uk/about-the-ico/what-we-do/legislation-we-cover/general-data-protection-regulation/ (Accessed 3rd March 2021).

Janis, I.L. (1982) *Groupthink: Psychological Studies of Policy Decisions and Fiascoes*, 2nd ed., Boston: Houghton Mifflin.

Kintish, W. (2014) *Business Networking: The Survival Guide*, Harlow: Pearson Education Limited.

52 The ethics of networking

Li, P.P., Zhou, S.S., Zhou, A.J. and Yang, Z. (2019) 'Reconceptualizing and Redirecting Research on Guanxi: "Guan-Xi" Interaction to Form a Multicolored Chinese Knot,' *Management and Organization Review* 15(3): 643–677, doi:10.1017/mor.2019.36

McGinn, K.L and Tempest, N. (2010) 'Heidi Roizen,' rev. ed. Available at: https://www.hbs.edu/faculty/Pages/item.aspx?num=26880 (Accessed 5th March 2021).

Melé, D. (2009) 'The Practice of Networking: An Ethical Approach,' *Journal of Business Ethics* 90(4): 487–503, doi: 10.1007/s10551-010-0602-2

Muller, M. (2013) 'Nestlé Baby Milk Scandal Has Grown Up But Not Gone Away,' *Guardian*, Wed 13 Feb [Online]. Available at: https://www.theguardian.com/sustainable-business/nestle-baby-milk-scandal-food-industry-standards#comments

Nicomachean Ethics, Book VIII. Aristotle, c. 350 BCE. Translated by W.D. Ross. [Online]. Available at: http://classics.mit.edu/Aristotle/nicomachaen.8.viii.html (Accessed 19th February 2021).

Rundall, P. (2021) 'The Code and Other Safeguards Threatened by Corporate Friendly Voluntary Guidelines on Food Systems and Nutrition,' Patti Rundall's policy blog, Baby Milk Action IBFAN UK, 4th February. [Online]. Available at: http://www.babymilkaction.org/archives/28207 (Accessed: 18th February 2021).

Schonsheck, J. (2000) 'Business Friends: Aristotle, Kant and Other Management Theorists on the Practice of Networking,' *Business Ethics Quarterly* 10(4): 897–910, doi: 10.2307/3857838.

Socratous, M. (2018) 'Networking: A Male Dominated Game,' *Gender in Management* 33(2): 167–183, doi: 10.1108/GM-11–2016–0181

Townsend, H. (2014) *Business Networking: How to Use the Power of Online and Offline Networking for Business Success*, 2nd ed., Harlow: Pearson Education Limited.

Wong, Y.H. and Chan, R.Y. (1999) 'Relationship Marketing in China: Guanxi, Favouritism and Adaptation,' *Journal of Business Ethics* 22(2): 107–118, doi: 10.1023/A:1006077210425

3

NETWORKING ACROSS ORGANISATIONAL BOUNDARIES

Introduction

This chapter looks specifically at the role of organisations set up to enable networking to occur: the reasons why networks are set up purposefully and how to optimise their success. Networks can take many forms, from the unboundaried and fairly inchoate forms of the personal networks of individual actors to highly structured and defined networks set up with a clear core mission. It is this latter type of network that is the subject of this present chapter, with a particular interest in network organisations whose mission is to speed up innovation. We will call these formal or managed networks. This chapter will consider:

- The reasons why such networks might be established
- Factors in their development, using a case study approach
- Enabling their success
- The practical implications for stakeholder management

Drawing on previously unpublished research, extended and developed with reference to recent literature, this chapter uses an extended large-scale case study to draw out lessons which are transferable to a wide range of cross-sector-managed networks. As this chapter is focused on the network at a structural level, it may be of particular value to network leaders or directors. Networking for social change at the level of the individual actor is covered in Chapter 5.

Networking and innovation

The literature on innovation emphasises the need for co-operation across sectors and against more traditional competitive market pressures, creating a policy

DOI: 10.4324/9781003026549-4

54 Networking organisational boundaries

> ### Viewpoint 3.1 Working across organisational boundaries
>
> I'll give you some really good examples about this because it's so contemporary; this is a space I'm living in at the moment. I could work across the health systems, have conversations with other providers about how we might manage an issue or topic or a problem that we're all facing into and there can be very open and safe conversations about that. For example, take the COVID vaccine campaign. We've got a cohort of housebound patients, an incredibly difficult vaccine to manage logistically. How do we square the two and get single doses of a multi-dose vaccine, that you can hardly breathe on without it destabilising, into individuals' homes? And the answer is, we're just not very well positioned to do that in primary care despite being asked to. The best people to do that are district nurses. So, we're talking to our community services colleagues about that and how we build the model and share some of the burden of the activity.

imperative to promote co-operation through the form of managed networks (Rampersad et al., 2010). Castells (2004, p. 5) identifies distinctive advantages to the network organisation versus more traditional organisational forms: taking advantage of new technologies, he suggests networks are flexible, scalable and able to survive. Flexibility first is derived from the fact that networks can change as the context changes, and can go round blockers more easily than more fixed organisational forms. Second, it is relatively easy for networks to grow or shrink in response to market pressures. Finally, because networks have no fixed centre and no permanent space or form and can act in multiple different configurations, they are uniquely well placed to survive and continue to perform even in hostile conditions. For these reasons, even in highly competitive markets, managed networks can serve a co-operative purpose where there is a mutual benefit in collaborative activity. Networking as a business activity is considered in the next chapter. Here, we are concerned with managed networks that are set up as mechanism of public policy, particularly those with an explicit mission to support innovation.

As in the private sector, there is a wider pressure in public services to become more innovative through collaboration (Hartley et al., 2013). Research suggests specific advantages to the collaborative approach compared to other methods of stimulating innovation, but there is a need to develop research which identifies when, where and why this is the best approach (Hartley, 2013; see Box 3.1). One extended study, for example, highlighted the problems with actor diversity and management activities in two case studies based in Finland (Aarikka- Stenroos et al., 2017). They discuss as a limitation to their work the problem of looking at just two cases (albeit in some depth and over time), and argue that more attention

BOX 3.1 ARE INNOVATION NETWORKS RELEVANT IN ALL INDUSTRY SECTORS?

This chapter concentrates on networks in the area of healthcare, which spans private, public and charitable sector organisations, linking local providers of health services with, for example, large-scale global pharmaceutical companies. To what extent can lessons from health be extended into other industrial sectors? Is talking about industrial sectors meaningful, when the value of networking crosses organisational and sector boundaries?

In a fascinating and far-ranging paper, Dr. Richard A.L. Jones of the University of Manchester examines this problem. He argues that innovation, supported by publicly funded innovation networks working differentially in different economic regions, is vital to reignite growth both in the UK and in other developed nations. He discusses the needs for 'clusters' and 'commons' in different regions, organised perhaps around 'translational research institutes' which could lead in 'creating new networks to promote innovation, to diffuse new technologies, and raising skills levels'. His examination of different kinds of innovation emphasises both the economic argument for investment and also its value to the common good, both locally and more widely. As he argues:

> Historically, the main driver for state investment in innovation has been defence. Today, the largest fraction of government research and development supports healthcare – yet this is not done in a way that most effectively promotes either the health of our citizens or the productivity of our health and social care system. Most pressingly, we need innovation to create affordable low carbon energy.
>
> More attention needs to be paid to the wider determinants of innovation – organisation, management quality, skills, and the diffusion of innovation as much as discovery itself. We need to focus more on the formal and informal networks that drive innovation – and in particular on the geographical aspects of these networks. They work well in Cambridge – why aren't they working in the North East or in Wales?
>
> *(Adapted from Jones, 2019, pp. 2–3)*

needs to be given to examining how exactly diversity in networks both complicates and facilitates innovation. Other studies suggest that cross–sector innovation is very specifically limited by its context and culture (see Ramos et al., 2013, and Box 3.2).

Here, we offer insights gained from hitherto unpublished work into the 17 Health Innovation and Education Clusters (HIECs) in the UK that operated

56 Networking organisational boundaries

> **BOX 3.2 THE FRENCH SYSTEM OF INDUSTRIAL INNOVATION**
>
> Public policies and institutions are important to understand the collective learning inside national frontiers. Our central hypothesis is that public policy plays a determinant role in the constitution of innovation systems, especially when the private sector is not strong enough to take the lead. Cooperation among industry is not natural, even within national borders. Government policy can create favourable conditions for this cooperation by playing an active role and by creating the missing links in the system. The French pattern of public intervention, usually called Colbertism, is quite illustrative of this issue.
>
> The role of government in this model is very wide and consists not only in regulating, but also in introducing new public actors and coordination mechanisms with the specific purpose of building up and strengthening industrial 'filières' in these sectors. This kind of policy involves important public research and development (R&D) funds. Besides, the government intervenes in the supply side by creating large sector-oriented firms, which are prime contractors and associated public R&D centres in charge of basic but mostly applied research. The private sector acts in a complementary fashion through equipment and parts suppliers and engineering services firms. The articulation between these institutions takes place within large technological programmes, whose aim is to pursue a catching-up strategy. In fact, since the private sector is mostly laggard, government policy fills up the empty space by introducing new public actors that are more capable of undertaking and organising innovation (from Furtado, 1997, pp. 1243–1244, 1247).

from 2010 to 2015, and covered all parts of England except for a small area on the Southeast coast. While the findings can be seen to corroborate rather than significantly differ from the findings of other studies, this work has the merit of covering a large number of actors over a significant period under the auspices of the National Health Service (NHS) in the UK. As such, it offers a range of practical insights into the realities of formal networks in support of the academic literature across both health care and other sectors. The research identifies a number of salient factors which appear to support effective local collaborative innovation, notwithstanding the warnings acknowledged above about the limitations imposed by context and culture.

Establishing and developing cross-sector collaborative innovation in the NHS in England[1]

The HIECs were the first major iteration of cross-sectoral partnerships to promote innovation for the benefit of patients in England, precursors to the current Academic Health Science Networks. The HIECs spanned nine of the ten NHS regions in England from 2010 to 2015. The purpose of the HIECs was:

> to enable high quality patient care and services by quickly bringing the benefits of research and innovation directly to patients.
>
> *(Darzi, 2008; Department of Health, 2009)*

borrowing from best practice in healthcare in other developed economies and from other industrial sectors in the UK.

Working across the system in a collaborative fashion requires very different skills and approaches to those deployed within the organisations that make up the collaboration (Alexander et al., 1998). Proponents of the collaborative approach argue that the introduction of a broad range of actors generates new understandings of the nature of the innovation process (Brommert, 2010). There are however inherent difficulties in developing such local collaborative networks, particularly when the network is cross-sectoral as the member organisations may have very different goals and system drivers. Networks such as the HIECs are based on voluntary collaboration rather than hierarchical control: they have a broad vision and mission; the partners are not equal in terms of their resources and their commitment; and the aims of individual collaborations may lead to varied outcomes from practical service changes to the development of new forms of knowledge (Alexander et al., 1998, 2001).

If broad cross-sector partnerships have a vague mandate from central government (Montjoy and O'Toole, 1979), they can struggle to define their purpose or to access sufficient resources to carry out their new mission. This is compounded by the potential for change over time, with new partners entering the arena or becoming active or inactive. Accountability can rest with multiple stakeholders: the partners in the network, funding agencies, policymakers more generally, patients and the public.

Furthermore, although the increase in formal networks across public services can be observed, it is difficult to assess their impact or their success, especially where the definition of their initial purpose was vague. In a systematic assessment of the critical variables which may produce successful collaboration, Ansell and Gash referred to:

> groping to find a common language of description and evaluation.
>
> *(Ansell and Gash, 2008, p. 549)*

The informality of many collaborations, which may be part of their real world success, makes them difficult to describe and analyse in ways that easily lend themselves to the evolution of theory.

Notwithstanding this acknowledged problem, Ansell and Gash conducted a meta-review of 137 examples of such networks, which led to the identification of five variables that they argue influence successful collaboration:

58 Networking organisational boundaries

- Prior history of conflict or cooperation
- Incentives for stakeholders to participate
- Power and resource imbalances
- Leadership
- Institutional design

A similar meta-review was carried out by Zakocs and Edwards (2006), who argue that despite the increasing emphasis on cross-sectoral working, there is still relatively little evidence about what makes such coalitions work. They accord with Ansell and Gash in identifying a number of serious methodological difficulties such as variability in conceptual definitions in the studies they select; problems in defining what is meant by individual factors such as leadership; and a problem in establishing the causal relationships between the different factors and network outcomes in terms of changes to community health outcomes.

In terms of the effectiveness of the functioning of the network or coalition, the evidence-based factors that emerged as most significant in their study (Zakocs and Edwards, 2006) were:

- Formalisation of rules/procedures/processes
- Leadership style
- Member participation
- Membership diversity
- Agency collaboration
- Group cohesion

The taxonomies developed in these two meta-reviews are supported by similar studies of cross-sectoral partnerships (Weiner and Alexander, 1998; Shortell et al., 2002; Alexander et al., 2003; Wells and Weiner, 2007) and therefore provide a useful framework for analysis. This framework provided a starting point for examining the formation, management and governance processes and the operations of the 17 HIECs. They can be combined and represented diagrammatically as follows (Figure 3.1).

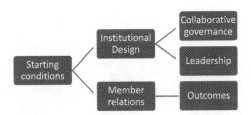

FIGURE 3.1 Establishing and developing cross-sector health innovation collaborations.

Lessons learnt from the Health Innovation and Education Clusters

The purpose of researching the experiences of the HIECs was to determine the factors which study participants considered important in establishing and developing the HIECs, and to capture learning to inform future cross-sector collaborations through managed networks.

Several themes emerged from the analysis: starting conditions, institutional design which incorporates both leadership and collaborative governance and member relations and outcomes were indicated by the literature and incorporated into the framework for analysis (Figure 3.1). Additionally, three novel themes emerged: first, time as a finite resource; second, sustainability; and third, definitions of success. Each of these themes is described below. Looking in more detail at a large-scale case study of managed networks, the best of which lasted over a five-year period, can give insights into how such networks flourish or founder.

1. *Starting Conditions*: 'We had a number of very traditional rivalries'

    All 17 HIECs formally came into being on 1 April 2010. However, progress differed between them in terms of how quickly they set up operations and began their work. This could be due to a number of factors such as the strength of the original bid, local experiences of working together, hosting arrangements and the speed with which a management team was put in place to pull the activities of the partnership together. In some localities, there was a pre-existing will to work more collaboratively:

    > I was fortunate in that I inherited a HIEC that has a very good respected team and leadership...and so some of that leg work was already done for me

    In other places, this was not so. Several HIECs reported on a strong local history of rivalry and a lack of collaboration, predating the arrival of the HIEC:

    > The rivalry between the teaching hospitals and the medical schools was significant.

    In a minority of cases, HIECs failed to counteract imbalances in power and influence ('Within our health economy we have one very, very large university hospital that is massive compared to the other two DGHs and it is considered the "big beast"').

    Disparities in scale or mission between constituent organisations were a significant issue in terms of building collaboration, and a considerable degree of time and creative ways of reaching out to all were deployed to try to counteract the impact of such imbalances. Frow et al. (2014) refer to these kinds of preconditions as 'mega-factors' that need to be understood and managed. In their helpful overview of strategic network theory, Möller

60 Networking organisational boundaries

and Halinen (2017) suggest that the individual agency of actors in the network (whether these are industry bodies, organisations or individuals) is a neglected area for research; too often, it is just accepted that one powerful player will dominate the network, without questioning whether or not this is an effective strategy for network formation. This may perhaps be a bigger problem in regulated sectors, such as health or law:

> A regulated sector is a complex sector and one in which change and dynamics tend to be slow moving. Actor positions, resources, activities, relationships and changes tend to be regulated as well, that is to say, not free to evolve, producing as a result the effect of constraining both relationships and the network. The final result of not sharing objectives is a general impoverishment of the system.
>
> *(Cantù et al., 2013, p. 1009)*

Viewpoint 3.2 Networking as mutual support when dealing with the NHS

I think it plays an important role for people from various companies dealing with the NHS to come together and say 'my God, this is just awful' so that sharing of despair is a comfort because it gives you the sense that we're all trying to fight this great beast. So, we're joined in that. That's what I'd... I describe as a social thing in the wider sense.

---

2. *Leadership*: 'My job was to do something different'

All HIECs had a small paid staff team, including a role described variously as Chief Executive or Managing Director. Boards were visible leaders in terms of strategy development, external relationship building and a visioning of new ways of working. While all respondents acknowledged that leadership was a critical factor in enabling HIEC partnerships to work, several felt that finding the right kind of leaders for a collaborative innovation context was difficult. The skills set required included working in non-hierarchical ways, being diplomatic and the ability to work with an unusually wide spread of different kinds of people. Persistence in the face of disappointment or setback and a willingness to use personal networks for the wider good were also important.

Matinheikki et al. (2017) examined two health care networks in Finland and came to a similar conclusion: that leaders of these kinds of networks are not managers in a traditional sense, but rather (Box 3.3):

> architects who facilitate shared decision making.
>
> *(Matinheikki et al., 2017, p. 130)*

BOX 3.3 LEARNING FROM FAILURE IN BELGIUM

During the period 2011–2012, efforts were made in the Belgium health economy (in common with many highly developed national healthcare systems) to mobilise all the significant players across the system to adopt radical innovation in the areas of heart failure and cancer, moving the system towards a far higher degree of personalised medicine. These efforts were largely unsuccessful. The authors of the case study used a 'thought experiment' methodology to capture the implicit perceptions, attitudes and intentions to act of the key stakeholders in the intended networks, identifying the significant players and analysing the structures of resistance to innovation.

They uncovered three tools to be used to improve mobilisation:

- Understanding higher order values
- Cultural proximity
- Maturity

By examining these factors in the local context, network managers can understand and work to improve the engagement of key players. Interestingly, the authors of the study identify a need to understand and manage optimism as a double-sided phenomenon:

> It is not only those neutral or skeptic stakeholders that need to be managed in a mobilization process, but over optimists as well. By charging into a field while they themselves lack credibility, the over-optimists risk entrenching the skeptics and undermining the more credible mobilization attempts.

> (p. 82)

> (Adapted from Van Brockhaven and Matthyssens, 2017)

3. *Collaborative governance*: 'the right organisations that would help us innovate'
   A key role of the Boards of the HIECs was setting clear and transparent processes for the ways they would work. Several respondents referred to the existence of such processes as one of the reasons for success:

> Any tensions were resolved through spending the time building the understanding about what was necessary and then, as a result of that, we were able to do more developed things between different sectors.

The critical relationship between the function of the Board as a formal governance mechanism and the collateral leadership the Board exercised in terms of establishing the partnership and the partnership working acted as a

62 Networking organisational boundaries

mechanism to build the credibility of the HIEC with the wider stakeholder community (Ovseiko et al., 2014). Some of the complexities of working collaboratively as well as providing clear governance oversight are explored by Vangen et al. (2015):

> The distinction between "collaborative governance" and "governing collaboration" also focuses attention on the kinds of management tensions that may arise and how they may be addressed. For example, it draws attention to the "efficiency and inclusiveness" tension, suggesting that the governance form needs a structure that is tight enough to allow for consensus-oriented decision-making yet open enough to ensure continuing inclusion of enough stakeholders to help sustain the collaboration over a period of time. And it points to a possible notion of "unobtrusive leadership": the idea that the governance form must support the inclusion of actors who are well recognized and accepted as leaders without their leadership being obviously visible or perceived by otherwise "equal" partners as interfering.
>
> (Vangen et al., 2015, p. 1258)

4. *Member relations*: 'A critical mass of committed people'

All HIECs had representation from different sectors of the NHS and from academia. Most HIECs worked to some extent with local government, industry and/or the charitable sector. When asked to indicate whether engagement from different sectors had been sufficient for HIECs to accomplish their objectives, one respondent commented:

> Given the scale of some of these sectors, we have done no more than scratch the surface.

However, there were some notable successes. Two HIECs engaged significant numbers of community pharmacists in a particular piece of work. Another reported:

> We had 150 GPs, who were initially the least collaborative group of people you have ever met, sharing data and working together

Participation in collaborative projects across the lifetime of the HIEC can be used as a proxy measure for cross-sector boundary spanning. In terms of persuading different kinds of people to participate in HIEC programmes, Boards are again seen as a key actor. Seventy-one per cent stated that their Boards 'fully' or 'partly' directed partner organisations to fulfil their responsibilities, suggesting a considerable degree of Board level involvement in the operations and outcomes of member activity. It seems that many organisations would not have moved beyond light touch engagement to a more active collaboration without encouragement from the senior leadership across the local system. Trust is developed when all parties are seen to be willing to participate beyond token support: such participation is effective in mobilising deeper engagement across the system.

A similar study in Portugal confirms the importance of 'anchor institutions', especially in the network formation stage (Ramos et al., 2013). Frow et al. (2014) suggest a typology of eight 'co-creation practices' which support the sharing of resources during collaborative activities and interactions:

> Manifestations of co-creation practices offer evidence of the type and strength of relationships, the extent to which there is interaction, and the sharing and accessing of resources, which contribute to the ecosystem's well-being.
>
> *(Frow et al., 2014, p. 35)*

Viewpoint 3.3 Coalitions of the willing

I was quite keen to look across departments, so 'who can influence this thing that we're trying to achieve?' Very few significant policy issues are single-Department. They are about people, so they generally cross quite a few. But also 'Who's doing the work? Who's the recipient of the work: and who can represent them?'. So, you know, third sector organisations, private sector providers, and across Departments. My networks tended to look more like that.

5. *Outcomes*: 'We got very slick at finding the willing people'

Working on a project was the main mechanism by which organisations who wished to participate in the HIEC were enabled to do so. The choice of project and the allocation of resource to it was a device to deliver the wider goal of cross-sectoral collaboration for innovation. This relates to an ambition, frequently cited by respondents, to develop a deeper cultural change, encouraging people to learn to work differently in the future in ways which would foster openness to further innovative practice. Alongside working across organisations at Board level, HIECs actively recruited front-line staff into collaborative activity, building on small scale incremental innovation to more ambitious work:

> It is not a bad idea to start small and think big... the people we worked with were the worker bees really, the people who did the work rather than working at a strategic level where a lot of the politics sometimes comes in

It seems there is a complex relationship between working together, collaborating on projects and network strength (Van Den Broek-Busstra et al., 2017). Real change on the front line demonstrates the possibility of further more complex change down the line. There is a balancing act that needs continually

64 Networking organisational boundaries

to be managed between persuading participation in activities which may be of no direct benefit to an organisation, while ensuring that in the long run, the majority of network members do perceive value in continuing engagement.

> the system-level goal determines the effectiveness of the whole network (collective gains), but the majority of network members need to perceive it as beneficial to themselves (self-interest gains). Thus, combining these interests seems to remain as one of the great managerial challenges of the network era.
>
> *(Matinheikki et al., 2017, p. 130)*

So far, as we have seen above, the factors supporting collaborative innovation in the HIEC context accord with the literature, with some distinctive ways in which the HIECs manifested these factors. This suggests that there are sufficient factors in the evolution of the HIECs which match other case studies, enabling us to assume their lessons are broadly generalisable beyond the context of health care. There are however other variables that seem to have been important to the HIECs, not generally reported in the literature, which merit further examination.

6. *Time as a finite resource*: 'A real sense of urgency'

The HIECs were a time-limited initiative, and their time scale for operations changed several times over their lifespan. A general uncertainty over future plans was a significant feature of HIEC formation. Most respondents reported a pressure to perform, which they experienced generally as healthy in that it led to a focus on delivery. This was countered by the view that shifting timescales hampered planning. Generally, respondents felt that the HIECs had achieved significant things in difficult circumstances.

Some respondents reported that one benefit to being time-limited was an ability to stand aside from some of the longer-term system changes that preoccupied others. This gives rise to an important question about the optimum time span for a network of this type, if its role is to act as a catalyst to the building of local collaborative innovation. The experience of the HIECs might suggest that shorter time horizons can act as an incentive to making rapid progress in relationship building, while inevitably focusing on activity with shorter timeframes for delivering outcomes.

7. *Sustainability*: 'An attempt to deliver change which is sustained when we are gone'

When asked about their 'principal legacy', 65% of respondents referred in some way to collaboration, network building or a:

> methodology of working in partnership across organisations and across economic sectors.

Respondents felt that a key distinguishing feature of the HIECs was the extent to which they created complex multi-agency working, albeit generally

Networking organisational boundaries **65**

in smaller-scale pieces of work, and that this way of working could potentially be transferred to bodies with greater resources.

The HIECs had broken down some unhelpful older working relationships and brought new partners into the collaborative arena. They had done this through being seen as a trusted intermediary. If the HIEC was a 'neutral space', it could act as a broker for groups who typically did not work together:

> I think we were a vehicle to pull people together and the other thing that people keep telling me, especially the industry colleagues, is that what worked was the fact that we were seen as the honest broker and that has been our key strength.

Almost all HIECs referred to this kind of collaboration as new in the location where they were working and as the legacy that they looked to hand on:

> I think of the legacy in terms of culture really...the issue for us was simply how does innovation get into practice...

Arguing for a legacy that remains once the managed network is gone requires letting go, and trusting that the relationships that have been developed through the period of formal work will be sustained in the locality and through shared interests after the specific missions of the network are concluded. Scott et al. (2018) suggest that this kind of approach to network sustainability requires examination through a 'complexity theoretic lens', which may be uncomfortable for some, but which allows for:

> new approaches that will not be entirely controllable, and that will entail some sense of uncertainty.
>
> (Scott et al., 2018, p. 1084)

8. *Definitions of success*: 'We were driven to want to be accountable'

The HIECs demonstrated accountability in a number of ways: the ways in which they allocated resources in line with their mission, the ways in which they reported back to local stakeholders and the ways in which they managed performance. Trust-based mechanisms and other informal agreement also existed alongside project plans:

> the focus has simply been to make the best use of those funds.

As with the governance arrangements themselves, Boards leant towards 'high trust low bureaucracy' methods of managing internal accountability. Measuring collaboration in its own right proved more difficult than measuring project outcomes:

> What you have really got to try and measure is the added value arising from collaborations... to demonstrate in some way [that] the projects

66 Networking organisational boundaries

> that we funded were novel in their cross–organisational cross–sector nature...

In discussing the problem of measuring success against more complex metrics, Head (2008) argues for the need for a learning improvement approach to:

> the capacity to demonstrate the benefits of collective investment and accountability for results.
>
> *(Head, 2008, p. 746)*

Transferable ideas from the HIEC networks

In summary, the experience of the 17 HIECs can be summarised into a number of points to attend to, in order to optimise success in setting up and running a managed network. These are:

- Understand the starting conditions and the history of collaboration or rivalry in the proposed group of members
- Appoint the right kind of leaders
- Support the leadership through appropriate trust-based governance mechanisms
- Build a critical mass of engaged individuals and organisations
- Build engagement through participation in shared projects
- Create a sense of urgency
- Think about legacy from the start
- Be accountable

Concluding this report into the activities and experiences of the HIECs, we have extended and adapted further the criteria identified initially from a review of the research literature to add in the extra success factors the HIECs reported as important to how their networks evolved (Figure 3.2). If other networks can find ways to incorporate these into their network design, we believe the chance that the network will be successful will be increased. The HIECs reported that their success was attributable, in part, to their short timespan which created a sense of urgency, their awareness of the need to build a sustainable legacy and their highly developed sense of accountability (derived, at least in part, in reaction to the early threat to survival). It is worth explicitly stating here that being accountable does not invalidate trust-based governance processes; rather, it reinforces a sense that all members share in the responsibility to be trustworthy.

This framework offers a method for thinking systematically about managed networks, the preconditions that affect their early days, the structural issues that might support collaboration in terms of leadership and governance and the expected lifespan and legacy. Thinking about these issues in the round will

FIGURE 3.2 Establishing and developing cross-sectoral health innovation collaborations (modified).

optimise the possibility that such networks are successful, something that tends to be underestimated in the policy formation that establishes them.

One contributor to the HIEC study observed:

> There is a fundamental lack of understanding…about the skills, time and effort that is required to make things happen in a complex system.

Implications for practice

The significance of this chapter from a practical perspective is the management of all the stakeholders in a potential innovation network, given that boundary spanning and working across organisations is a clear feature of them. We have seen from studying such networks that power imbalances and historically poor relationships can impede their development, while time, trust and leadership contribute to growth and success. The practical challenge therefore is to identify and understand the differing perspectives of stakeholders and then to manage them actively in order to harness their efforts positively to the wider benefit of the whole network.

In terms of categorising the types of stakeholder involved, we suggest the use of the framework we advance in Chapter 1 as a possible starting point here (Figure 3.3):

In the first instance, stakeholders can be categorised by what you know of their conscious reasons for joining the network. The different actors will have more or less engagement, and therefore the network organisers may have greater or more limited understanding of individuals' avowed intentions for joining. We would suggest that understanding the differing starting points is a key need for the early stages of formation. Furthermore, it is helpful to know how strongly the key individuals feel about being involved to gain a sense of their likely evolving influence. Information on members' reasons for joining can be sought through a variety of means: face-to-face meetings, informal surveys and frequency of interactions (i.e. by logging attendance at events, or participation in digital fora etc.).

68 Networking organisational boundaries

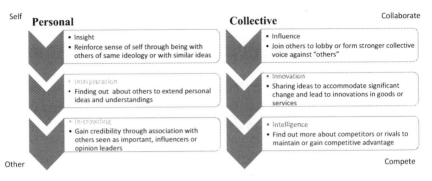

FIGURE 3.3 The network-IN model (repeated).

In the early days, the network may benefit particularly from those members who are drawn to it by either a genuine desire to extend and widen their own knowledge or by those who come with a clear focus on innovation ideally strengthened by organisational support for participation. In our model, we call these kinds of motivation IN-terpretation and IN-novation and their definitions are included here for convenience.

> ### Viewpoint 3.4 Learning from others
>
> I had a conversation yesterday, for example, where somebody who I'm going to bring into the business again in the New Year who ran a couple of sessions for us during the summer on the whole issue of well-being, resilience and coping with lockdown and remote working and… and all of those wonderful things that are challenges to working practices and… and well-being at the moment.
>
> We exchanged about 45 minutes of conversation about the things that I was seeing and the things that she was seeing. So, we were feeding into each other's perspectives. I probably wouldn't instantly have thought about that as networking. But we were definitely feeding into each other's thought processes. I think that's a fundamental part of business interface and collaborative working

- *Interpretation*: Others focus more on their personal learning, wishing to associate with others whom they consider are dealing with similar issues to themselves, or alternatively, to increase their understanding of individuals with different backgrounds who share a common purpose. The primary outcome sought here is an extension of personal ideas and understandings, helping to develop a deeper understanding of the world they inhabit.

Networking organisational boundaries **69**

- *Innovation*: Some people will seek out networks with a membership from people with very different backgrounds to their own, with an explicit aim of sharing ideas that can lead to innovation in products or services, often at times of significant change. These people may join such networks with a mandate from their employer or the interest group they represent.

Viewpoint 3.5 Sharing ideas for innovation

Some years ago, we did directly get business out of that, with a pharmaceutical company doing patient support programmes and actually over the years that was quite a lot of money for us. And that was directly as a result of a guy from a pharmaceutical company being at the meeting; me having the opportunity to say what we did, and then getting talking. So that was a direct, commercially valuable outcome for us of that networking event. There were other things that came out of that; other clinical groups saying 'what are your interests?', 'what are you doing?' This area, say COPD, and asthma, your lungs: 'well, that's interesting'.

The reason for an initial focus on these kinds of people is that they will have expressed an explicit motivation to engage, and they are less likely to be motivated by wishing to get something back, either personally or for their organisation, than some others in our typology. Lynch (2008) suggests that stakeholders are mapped against those who will carry out strategy and those who have a stake in the outcomes. We would adapt this rather more simply in the early stages of network formation to mapping two axes:

- The doers
- The blockers

So, in very informal terms, stakeholders can be mapped in this way (Figure 3.4).

The 'Foreign powers' may be located at some distance from the network and have little concern with its day-to-day activities. However, most probably through the allocation of resources, they do have the power to block or control activities with which they are not happy. It is important therefore to manage them through regular formal communications and processes of accountability.

Below them is the group called 'Friends', who are deemed to have little power or interest in blocking activities, but equally are too busy or too distant to wish to have much involvement in the activities of the network. It is important to keep a general communication out to this group on a regular basis, so they feel in touch, as they may move to one or other group given the dynamic nature of networks.

A critically important group to network success are the 'worker bees', who will actively involve themselves in innovation activities and deliver the changes required on the ground. These people will be the greatest asset to the network,

70 Networking organisational boundaries

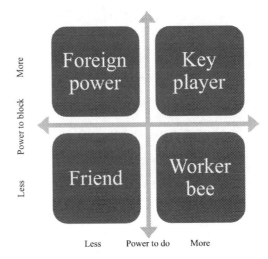

FIGURE 3.4 Network stakeholder model.

even though they lack the ability to exercise power or block achievements. It is important not to underestimate the groundswell of positivity that can come from the front line, and to remember to give credit to the contributions of those who trial, experiment and operationalise the projects and activities of the networks. These people will be strongly motivated by their personal wish to gain knowledge through collaboration, and thus they will be willing to interpret the understandings gained to their peers.

Viewpoint 3.6 Doers and blockers

Nurses by and large are easier [to work with] because frankly you can talk about patients. They're the ones who are in contact with the patients 'all the time', in inverted commas. The consultants don't see the patients that often. So that you can talk about particular patients with nurses which you could never do with a higher-level clinician. I've sat in meetings with professors who give me their views on my technology. I'm quite welcome and very open to how my technology does or does not meet your needs. But I'm not going to be spoken to by some professor of 'what's it' about whether this particular way of running a system or holding a database is correct. That's my job, mate, I do this for a bloody living.

Finally, the group known as 'key players' have both the power to block activities and also the power to mobilise resources to support intended network outcomes. Unlike the 'foreign powers', they do have the intention of getting involved but may well not be initially supportive of some or all of the network missions. Historical factors in the locality can influence the conscious or unconscious decisions of these players, especially with regard to resources and decisions on organisational structure, governance and operations. Nonetheless, this is the group of innovators who, once actively engaged, will yield the greatest benefits, especially at the start.

All the stakeholders need strategies to manage them but the role of the leadership, in the early days, will be particularly directed towards the key players. The lessons of the HIECs suggest that these individuals can become significant resources to the network, but it is important to recognise the prehistory and existing relationships which will be impacting on their thinking, even if they are not necessarily willing to say so.

These kinds of decisions, about where to direct the leadership effort in the early days, are guided by the concept of 'stakeholder salience'. To help distinguish between the different kinds of key players, it is helpful to apply a framework developed by Mitchell et al. in 1997. This distinguishes between three forms of stakeholder salience: power, legitimacy and urgency. Power, as we have seen, is concerned with the ability to block progress and equally to support and promote the mission of the network.

Legitimacy is about the credibility of an organisation in terms of network influence, for example, in a health care network, this would apply to a large teaching hospital (e.g. the 'big beast' described by one of the HIECs above). In terms of managed networks, all players can be seen as legitimate as, by definition, such networks cut across traditional sectors and hierarchies. But it must be acknowledged that some of these actors are seen as being more credible by the other members, by virtue of their scale, status or reputation.

Finally, urgency relates to the variable of time which we have considered as significant for networks – a sense of wishing to press on through network formation to effective operations and thus meaningful outcomes. This can bring real energy to the group, so this is how we describe it in terms of our adaptation of Mitchell's (1997) framework to the context specifically of networks (Figure 3.5):

Those with power, energy and credibility are the key players that need to be identified and harnessed in the initial stages of network formation. In the quotation cited above, in referring to a highly dominant figure in their network as a 'big

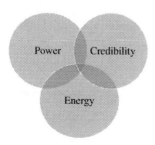

FIGURE 3.5 Network saliency model.

72 Networking organisational boundaries

beast', they tacitly acknowledge that differentials in power and status are often a factor in network formation. If the biggest beasts in our network jungle are those who possess power, energy and credibility, who else is there too? Metaphor is a powerful tool in thinking about management (Chowdury, 2021) and the concept of an ecosystem, teeming with wildlife of various species, can bring our stakeholder analysis to life. Those with power alone may not choose to exercise it – they are the 'sleeping lions' who should be left alone until they wake. In the same way, stakeholders who have energy alone may have relatively low salience for the networks – they are the 'humming birds' who are decorative and may demand a certain amount of attention from the network, but not necessarily key players. They matter too though, as they will attract attention from others and should not be seen to be neglected; perhaps a critical group as the network moves past its early formation and into some 'doing' activities, an injection of energy may be what is needed at that point.

The credible players are our 'great apes' – intelligent and awesome, but like the gorilla may keep aloof from the network. Where the circles overlap, there is greater salience: those with 'power' and 'energy' are dangerous like the mighty rhino; where the gazelles, with urgency and credibility on their side, lack the resource power to exert much influence on the network; and the dominant tigers will exert their power and credibility to ensure they are not overlooked. Once each of the stakeholder 'beasts' has been identified, it is then important to develop a detailed strategy to find a role for each one.

Breaking down the players into these categories, while light-hearted, may help all these key players to add value to the network in their distinctive ways. Effective network management sees the value in managing all stakeholders and in using individual actors in ways which matches their intrinsic motivations to the needs of the network. Finally, it is important too to remember that motivation can change over time for a whole variety of reasons – in this jungle, the leopards may change their spots.

Conclusion

We have used the term 'managed networks' to consider any kind of network set up with a mandate from a public policymaker of some sort, and therefore with an end which is not entirely defined or shaped by the network members. As we have seen with our lengthy case study, which provides a shape to discuss the issues that arise from such a mandate, simply requiring collaboration does not guarantee its delivery. Despite the variety of forms, shapes and scale in which managed networks may arise, they will grapple with some common challenges. In this chapter, we have suggested some of the factors that affect collaboration: to create boundary spanning relationships, encourage engagement and assure trust in the outcomes delivered. These are some of the factors that require attention. The ways that these factors are then managed, alongside other factors that may arise locally, are contingent on both culture and context. There is no road map to guarantee success. There are however some milestones to attend to, on the road to successful collaboration.

Viewpoint 3.7 Maintaining engagement

I think, because of the sort of work that I do, there's no received wisdom. It's constantly exploring new things: because lot of it is about business transformation and building different ways of doing things and building different approaches and being agile and responsive. I'm always on the lookout for different ways of seeing things and approaching things.

Networking narratives

3. A perspective from a network leader

I think clarity of purpose is important and then making sure that you recruit the network participants around whatever that vision is: and that the people have shared values, and share that vision.

Managed networks do suffer from a lack of clarity in the first place and I think that then leads into a lack of engagement. That's the biggest difficulty of running any network. I think it's a cultural thing. The culture in this country is that we are a nation of joiners. People like joining things. So, it's not too difficult to recruit people to your network, but the difficult thing is to get them to engage and get them to participate. As a rule of thumb, if you engage 20% of your membership you're doing very well and usually the active participation is about 10%, but that's not to say that other people don't get anything out of it.

The problem with setting metrics is that nobody really knows what engagement means. With professional membership organisations, for example, the only metric you've got is people renewing their subscriptions as to whether they're getting anything out of it or not.

We put in a bid at the Regional Development Agency for quite a substantial grant to form an innovation hub. The four parties who were obviously the key people we needed to get to be part of this, traditionally just did not talk to each other and actually openly hated each other. We had to get them in a room and force them to start talking to each other. We won the bid, and then they worked together. But of course, they would never admit afterwards that they'd been in such a position that they couldn't be in the same room together before we had physically got them to do that. So, I think that the facilitation aspect is another element of what makes a good network.

It goes back to facilitation again, effectively having a strong chair who will bring all these people together and make sure that the voices are heard of the... of the people who are quietest and the voices of the larger organisations are not unduly influential. So, it's that strong facilitation part.

74 Networking organisational boundaries

> But it also comes down to this thing about engagement, in that you will not get the views of everyone until you do something terribly wrong in their eyes. So, the views that you normally get will be the minority, the disaffected or whatever, which is what happens with patients. But I think some of the initiatives that have gone into training patients how to advocate for themselves or how to take part have proved to be very effective in bringing in the minority voice, and empowering it by training them into how to take part in a network. In Bristol, they set up a sort of Learning Academy for patient voice. People who had a particular disease or illness or whatever would go along to these things, and have sessions on how they can make themselves aware, and how they can use their voice and also how they can draw in the views of other people and not just be a single illness advocate.

Ask yourself?

1. What is the difference between engagement and participation? Where would you place yourself on that continuum?
2. What attributes is the speaker describing in terms of network leadership?
3. What steps can be taken to build shared values in a network?
4. What practical steps can be taken to solicit the views of different kinds of members, without waiting until things go wrong?

Note

1 This chapter draws, in part, on hitherto unpublished research carried out as part of a study into network governance undertaken in 2013–2014 in Oxford, UK. The outcomes of the study were published by Ovseiko et al. (2014). This chapter contains extra material relating to the formation, operations and legacy of the HIECs, which have hitherto been unreported and which here are extended and developed by new insights, both from more recent published research and from the empirical work carried out in preparation for this book. Thanks are due to Dr. Susan C. Powell, Centre for Innovation and Knowledge Exchange, Manchester Metropolitan University, and Dr. Pavel C. Ovseiko, Medical Sciences Division, University of Oxford. The study gained ethical approval from the University of Oxford Ethics Committee (MSD_IDREC_C1_2012-160).

References

Aarikka-Stenroos, L., Jaakkola, E., Harrison, D. and Makitalo-Keinonen, T. (2017) 'How to Manage Innovation Processes in Extensive Networks: A Longitudinal Study,' *Industrial Marketing Management*, 67: 88–105, http://dx.doi.org/10.1016/j.indmarman.2017.09.014

Alexander, J.A., Comfort, M.E. and Weiner, B.J. (1998) 'Governance in Public-Private Community Health Partnerships: A Survey of the Community Care Network[SM] Demonstration Sites,' *Nonprofit Management and Leadership*, 8(4): 311–332, doi: 10.1002/nml.8402

Alexander, J.A., Comfort, M.E., Weiner, B.J. and Bogue, R. (2001). 'Leadership in Collaborative Community Health Partnerships,' *Nonprofit Management and Leadership*, 12(2): 159–175, doi: 10.1002/nml.12203

Alexander, J.A., Weiner, B.J., Metzger, M.E., Shortell, S.M., Bazzoli, G.J., Hasnain-Wynia, R., Sofaer, S. and Conrad, D.A. (2003). 'Sustainability of Collaborative Capacity in Community Health Partnerships,' *Medical Care Research and Review*, 60(4 Suppl): 130S–160S, doi: 10.1177/1077558703259069

Ansell, C. and Gash, A. (2008) 'Collaborative Governance in Theory and Practice,' *Journal of Public Administration Research and Theory* 18(4): 543–571, doi: 10.1093/jopart/mum032

Brommert, B. (2010) 'Collaborative Innovation in the Public Sector,' *International Public Management Review* 11(1): 15–33.

Cantu, C., Corsaro, D., Fiocca, R. and Tunisini, A. (2013) 'IMP Studies: A Bridge between Tradition and Innovation,' *Industrial Marketing Management* 42: 1007–1016, http://dx.doi.org/10.1016/j.indmarman.2013.07.021

Castells, M. (ed) (2004) *The Network Society: A Cross-Cultural Perspective*, Cheltenham: Edward Elgar.

Chowdhury, R. (2021) 'An Appreciation of Metaphors in Management Consulting from the Conceptual Lens of Holistic Flexibility,' *Systems Research and Behavioral Science* 38(1): 137–157. doi: 10.1002/sres.2670.

Darzi A. (2008) *High Quality Care For All: NHS Next Stage Review Review Final Report. Volume Cm7432*, London: Department of Health, www.dh.gov.uk/en/Publicationsandstatistics/Publications/PublicationsPolicyAndGuidance/DH_085825

Department of Health: Breakthrough to Real Change in Local Healthcare: A Guide for Applications to Create Health Innovation and Education Clusters (HIECs).(2009), http://www.dh.gov.uk/en/Publicationsandstatistics/Publications/PublicationsPolicyAndGuidance/DH_098887

Frow, P., McColl-Kennedy, J.R. and Payne, A. (2016) 'Co-Creation Practices: Their Role in Shaping a Health Care Ecosystem,' *Industrial Marketing Management* 56: 24–39, http://dx.doi.org/10.1016/j.indmarman.2016.03.007

Furtado, A. (1997) 'The French System of Innovation in the OIl Industry: Some Lessons About the Role of Public Policies and Sectoral Patterns of Technological Change in Innovation Networking,' *Research Policy* 25: 1243–1259, PH S0048–7333(96)00907-9

Hartley, J., Sorensen, E. and Torfing, J. (2013) 'Collaborative Innovation: A Viable Alternative to Market Competition and Organisational Entrepreneurship,' *Public Administration Review* 73(6): 821–830, doi: 10.1111/puar.12136

Head, B. (2008) 'Assessing Network-Based Collaborations,' *Public Management Review* 10(6): 733–749, https://doi.org/10.1080/14719030802423087

Jones, R.A.L. (2019) *A Resurgence of the Regions: Rebuilding Innovation Capacity Across the Whole UK*. preprint. Available at http://www.softmachines.org/wordpress/?p=2340

Lynch, R. (2008) *Strategic Management*, 5th ed., Harlow: Financial Times/Prentice Hall.

Matinheikki, J., Pesonen, T., Artto, K. and Peltokorpi, A. (2017) 'New Value Creation in Business Natworks: The Role of Collective Action in Constructing System-Level Goals,' *Industrial Marketing Management* 67: 122–133, http://dx.doi.org/10.1016/j.indmarman.2017.06.011

Mitchell, R.K., Agle, B.R. and Wood, D.J. (1997) 'Toward a Theory of Stakeholder Identification and Salience: Defining the Principle of Who and What Really Counts,' *The Academy of Management Review* 22(4): 853–886, doi: 10.2307/259247

Möller, K. and Halinen, A. (2017) 'Managing Business and Innovation Networks- from Strategic Nets to Business Fields and Ecosystems,' *Industrial Marketing Management* 67: 5–22, https://doi.org/10.1016/j.indmarman.2017.09.018

76 Networking organisational boundaries

Montjoy, R.S. and O'Toole, L.J. (1979) 'Toward a Theory of Policy Implementation – Organizational Perspective,' *Public Administration Review* 39(5): 465–476, doi: 10.2307/3109921

Ovseiko, P.V., O'Sullivan, C., Powell, S.C., Davies, S.M. and Buchan, A.M. (2014) 'Implementation of Collaborative Governance in Cross-sector Innovation and Education Networks: Evidence from the National Health Service in England,' *BMC Health Services Research* 14: 552, doi: 10.1186/1472-6963-14-S2-P91

Ramos, C., Roseira, C., Brito, C., Henneberg, S. and Naudé, P. (2013) 'Business Service Networks and Their Process of Emergence: The Case of the Health Cluster Portugal,' *Industrial Marketing Management* 42: 950–968, http://dx.doi.org/10.1016/j.indmarman.2013.04.003

Rampersad, G., Quester, P. and Troshani, I. (2010) 'Managing Innovation Networks: Exploratory Evidence from ICT, Biotechnology and Nanotechnology Networks,' *Industrial Marketing Management* 39(5): 793–805.

Scott, A., Woolcott, G., Keast, R. and Chamberlain, C. (2018) 'Sustainability of Collaborative Networks in Higher Education Research Projects: Why Complexity? Why Now?' *Public Management Review* 20(7): 1068–1087, https://doi.org/10.1080/1471903 7.2017.1364410

Shortell, S.M., Zukosi, A.P., Alexander, J.A., Bazzoli, G.J., Conrad, D.A., Hasnain-Wynia, R., Sofaer, S., Chan, B.Y., Casey, E. and Margolin, F.S. (2002) 'Evaluating Partnerships for Community Health improvement; Tracking the Footprints,' *Journal of Health Politics, Policy and Law* 27(1): 49–91.

Van Bockhaven, W. and Matthyssens, P. (2017) 'Mobilizing a Network to Develop a Field: Enriching the Business Actor's Mobilisation Analysis Toolkit,' *Industrial Marketing Management* 67: 70–87, http://dx.doi.org/10.1016/j.indmarman.2017.08.001

Van den Broek-Busstra, L. Moolenaar, N.M. and De Groot, E. (2017) 'Knowledge Sharing in Interdisciplinary Networks of Health Care Professionals,' Presentation at *Third European Conference on Social Networks*, Mainz, September 2017.

Vangen, S., Hayes, J.P. and Cornforth, C. (2015) 'Governing Cross-Sector, Inter-Organizational Collaborations,' *Public Management Review* 17(9): 1237–1260, https://doi.org/10.1080/14719037.2014.903658

Weiner, B.J. and Alexander, J.A. (1998) 'The Challenges of Governing Public-Private Community Health Partnerships,' *Health Care Managment Review* 23(2): 39–55, doi: 10.1097/00004010-199804000-00005

Weiner, B.J., Alexander, J.A. and Zuckerman, H.S. (2000) 'Strategies for Effective Management Participation in Community Health Partnerships,' *Health Care Management Review* 25(3): 48–66, doi: 10.1097/00004010-200007000-00007

Wells, R. and Weiner, B.J. (2007) 'Adapting a Dynamic Model of Interorganizational Cooperation to the Health Care Sector,' *Medical Care Research and Review* 64(5): 518–543, doi: 10.1177/1077558707301166

Winstanley, D.D., Sorabji, S. and Dawson S. (1995) 'When the Pieces Don't fit: A Stakeholder Power Matrix to Analyse Public Sector Restructuring,' *Public Money and Management* 15(2): 19–26, doi: 10.1080/09540969509387865

Zakocs, R.C. and Edwards, E.M. (2006) 'What Explains Community Coalition Effectiveness?: A Review of the Literature,' *American Journal of Preventive Medicine* 30(4): 351–361.

4

NETWORKING FOR BUSINESS GROWTH

Introduction

The purposeful building and managing of relationships to grow or improve business or services is as relevant to the health of organisations as it is to the careers of people working in them. Organisations grow or shrink depending on how they recognise, create and exploit opportunities. Networking at a corporate level can be a route to growth by revealing such opportunities, developing existing ones and deciding which ones to reject or decommit from. Just as individuals need to weigh the potential benefit of networking against the time and opportunity cost involved, so organisations need to evaluate the role and relevance of networking to their growth strategies and allocate, develop and acquire resources as appropriate. This chapter looks at:

- The potential advantages to be gained from networking activities that take place between organisations
- How organisations can best position themselves to benefit from networking, including facilitating internal networking among their own employees

Definitions of organisational networking

The focus of much academic research in networking has been on activity at an individual, interpersonal level. Forret and Dougherty (2001) define it as:

> 'individuals' attempts to develop and maintain relationships with others who have the potential to assist them in their work or career.
>
> *(Forret and Dougherty, 2001, p. 284)*

DOI: 10.4324/9781003026549-5

78 Networking for business growth

More recently, evaluating the effect of networking activity on individual career success, Wolff and Moser (2009) conceptualise it as:

> behaviors that are aimed at building, maintaining, and using informal relationships that possess the (potential) benefit of facilitating work-related activities of individuals by voluntarily granting access to resources and maximizing common advantages.
>
> *(Wolff and Moser, 2009, pp. 196–197)*

Synthesising earlier definitions, Gibson et al. (2014) continue the emphasis on the interpersonal level in their definition of networking as:

> a form of goal-directed behavior, both inside and outside of an organization, focused on creating, cultivating, and utilizing interpersonal relationships.
>
> *(Gibson et al., 2014, p. 150)*

The definition we have adopted for the purposes of this book, as set out in Chapter 1, acknowledges the interpersonal and individual context of networking, but highlights a parallel organisational dimension in the role of networking for business growth and improvement:

> the purposeful building and managing of relationships to grow or improve business or services; to spread and promote ideas and ideals; or to support personal and career development.

This definition highlights how relationships exist at both organisational and individual levels, and implies the need for organisations to assess the benefits of networking activity at a corporate level, and to establish appropriate policies and controls to manage it effectively.

Viewpoint 4.1 It works for business development

It's a way for people working in similar sectors or with certain overlapping interests to get together to get to know each other, to help refer business, to help tackle problems that might need a multidisciplinary team, and in my case as a trading consultant, very much an opportunity for building a client base, expanding my business and potentially business development for colleagues as well – so you get that cross fertilisation. I think it does work for business development. All of the new business I've got has been through either referrals, people I already knew; or specific networking in this biotech Golden triangle sector. I haven't got anything from other networks.

Is networking good for business?

On the face of it, having managers who are good at networking at a personal level might be expected to result in successful, growing organisations. As long ago as 1982, the American management scholar John Kotter advocated 'network building' as a key management activity: –interacting with others in meetings, exchanging information and engaging with a wide range of contacts inside and outside the organisation. Such activity and the internal and external networks it produces allow managers to carry out their plans and responsibilities, their 'agenda' in Kotter's phrase (Kotter, 1982, p. 78).

In contrast, Luthans (1988) argued that a propensity for networking and managerial effectiveness is at odds with one another in practice. In a major observational study, published the same year (Luthans et al., 1988), Luthans et al. found that most managers who shine at networking are relatively ineffective at managing, as measured by the productivity and morale of the people reporting to them. They classified managerial activity into four streams: communication, resource allocation, human resource management and networking. Of these, networking is the only one for which they found a correlation with individual career progression. Luthans himself characterises networking somewhat negatively as:

> non-work related "chit-chat"; informal joking around; discussing rumors, hearsay and the grapevine; complaining, griping and putting others down; politicking and gamesmanship; dealing with customers, suppliers and vendors; attending external meetings; and doing/attending community service events.
>
> *(Luthans, 1988, p. 129)*

He bemoans the injustice and organisational inefficiency of socially adept managers being promoted over the heads of more technically competent but self-effacing peers.

But while Luthans's concept of networking includes time-wasting and trivialities, it also covers key drivers of organisational growth: the external relationships with customers, suppliers and other important stakeholders on which winning and maintaining business depends. Categorising a range of activities, both negative and positive, under one heading implies that Luthans considered them to be aspects of the same basic process. Perhaps it helps to be a bit of a politician and a gossip if you regularly deal with customers and suppliers? Perhaps your ability to spot a new business opportunity for your organisation is sharpened by a sense of what it might do for your career as an individual? Luthans (1988) concedes that some managers can be both successful and effective, balancing excellence across all four management activities; but fewer than 10% of his sample managed this combination. While we might expect the practice of management to have developed in the decades since Luthans's work was published, his ambivalence

80 Networking for business growth

about networking is an encouragement to take a critical view of its influence on business growth, whatever it might do for individual career progression.

This might appear to be counter-intuitive. For example, surely it is no more than common sense to expect personal networking by small business owners or professional service providers to result in new customers and contracts? Watson (2007) notes the relative absence of conclusive empirical evidence from previous research that it does, at least in a directly demonstrable fashion. Reassuringly, his longitudinal studies of the outcomes of networking for small- and medium-sized Australian businesses confirm a positive association with firm survival and growth (Watson, 2007, 2011). However, he found that growth only correlates with what he termed 'formal' networking with business services providers such as accountants or consultants (a contractual relationship that would stretch our definition of networking). Watson could not establish a correlation between networking of any kind and profitability, however. Relatively low profits might be expected for rapidly growing businesses establishing new markets, but Watson's findings are a useful counterbalance to the idea that networking activity is always a good thing from a business point of view. He provides surprisingly precise advice to business owners/managers, cautioning them against overextending their networks (accessing a maximum of six a year) and advising them to draw on any one network no more than three times a year (Watson, 2007, p. 870). More than this, the owner is unlikely to be spending enough time and attention on the main task of running their business.

The picture from our research was mixed with regard to the role of networking in business growth. Some respondents saw networking as integral to their new business development, and in one case actively promoted it in their organisation through training other staff. But even entrepreneurs who endorsed its business development value produced relatively few examples of efficacy in practice. The majority verdict was that networking activity helped establish an environment for sales rather than resulting in identifiable new business. Indirect effects are still effects, of course, but they make networking for business growth a difficult activity to evaluate, justify and plan for. This underlines the need for all organisations, from start-ups to large corporations, to adopt a conscious approach to networking and develop policies appropriate to their own contexts. As in management in general, it is practically impossible to provide universal principles. Even the effect of networking on individual careers has been shown to be highly context-dependent, varying with the extent to which a job role can be carried out autonomously or requires resources and input from others (Orpen, 1996). Its effects on growth at a corporate level are similarly contingent on other conditions, such as life stage of organisation, industry dynamics and the wider economic situation.

This chapter will look at how theory in two areas of business (marketing and strategy) can help us understand what is going on in networking at an organisational level and suggest principles for successful networking activity in this context. There is no 'one-size-fits-all' approach to networking that will work

Networking for business growth **81**

for every kind of organisation in every situation. But by using the frameworks in this chapter, managers can gain perspective on the challenges and opportunities of organisational networking and develop appropriate ways of addressing them. What follows is in two sections: the first drawing on marketing theory and the second on research on strategic capabilities and their role in organisational success.

Viewpoint 4.2 Managing my personal networks in search of business

If it's a contact or a business that I want to target again in six months' time, I'll keep an eye on the wires. I'll keep an eye on publications and send them a note saying 'I guess you read this – isn't this interesting?' Or 'Are they competitors of yours or potential future competitors? And, if so, do you need a quick analysis of the landscape?' And so I'm just dropping in little comments saying: 'don't forget me; if you need some help with that, I'm here'.

I did have a time, not last year but the year before, I had a terrible year with really zero clients, I was more active. So, I'd go to more meetings, meet more people. Because I needed to be… I was trying to build up the client base again.

Marketing perspectives on networking for business growth

A variety of schools of thought about the nature of marketing have developed alongside its growth as an academic discipline and management speciality (Hollander et al., 2005). Bagozzi (1974) was an early advocate of exchange theory, which understands marketing as essentially concerned with managing exchanges between two or more parties, each of whom has something of value to trade. In many respects, this is what is going on in a networking relationship, though usually over a considerably longer time frame than might be the case in a typical marketing exchange. Bagozzi emphasised the importance of communication, trust and respect in exchanges, resulting in the sustainable delivery of mutual benefit. Later writers have developed this view into a philosophy of marketing that sees enduring exchange relationships rather than individual transactions as the primary source of value in marketing (Gummesson, 1995).

Relationship marketing, as this approach is termed, underlines the relationship between supplier and buyer as the context for value creation rather than focusing on individual transactions. But the real value of such relationships becomes clear when seen as parts of wider networks, including other customers, suppliers and stakeholders. Again, this provides a clear analogy with accepted notions of networking, where your value as a network member increases with your ability to connect otherwise isolated nodes (Burt, 2004).

82 Networking for business growth

Organisations therefore need to manage long-term relationships not just on a one-to-one basis, but also as strategically embedded in networks of customers, suppliers and collaborators in a shifting pattern of value creation and appropriation. The costs and benefits of building and managing relationships between organisations will fluctuate according to changes in the larger networks of which such relationships are part. This is a considerable challenge for managers. It commits them to constant scanning of their far environments to detect change early as well as keeping sensitised to developments closer to home in their network contacts.

The complex interlaced nature of modern economies means that networking is an inescapable condition of business. Hakansson and Ford (2002) analyse three management paradoxes or dilemmas that network membership creates, each with practical implications for networking activity.

- *Balancing opportunity with constraint*: Network connections can lead to growth, but also limit freedom. The resources devoted to developing one set of relationships cannot be simultaneously invested in another. The more relationships connect an organisation into a network, the more opportunities and opportunity costs that organisation faces. Regular environmental scanning as mentioned previously and actions aimed at understanding the perspectives of other members can mitigate the risk of being locked into suboptimal relationships.
- *Influencing and being influenced*: Network membership implies an openness to innovation, ideas and influence. Less obviously influential network members can make their voices heard by focusing on the unique value they bring to their relationships. This is analogous to Porter's (1985) advice to firms to develop a unique market position that customers find compelling. Individuals and smaller organisations can wield disproportionate influence in a network by providing what members cannot find elsewhere. Those able to bridge 'structural holes' (Burt, 2004), that is, the gaps between otherwise well-connected network members, provide a good example. Their access to new ideas earns them attention and esteem in the network. While Burt's research was on internal networking by managers within a large electronics company, the principle extends to how influence works in networks of organisations.
- *Acceptance versus control*: Managed networks exist for various purposes (as discussed in Chapter 3) and marketing supply chains (which have many characteristics of networks) have a dominant member by virtue of ownership, contracts or simply economic power (Kotler et al., 2017, p. 347). However, Hakansson and Ford (2002) advise that as soon as organisations:

> acquire some "final" control over the surrounding network (or their supply chain or value chain!) they should be worried!
>
> *(Hakansson and Ford, 2002, pp. 138–139, punctuation in original)*

Individual members will naturally try to seek benefits such as business growth from the network. Such intentions imply an ambition to control events and environments to some extent. But the benefits of network membership (even, to a large extent, of managed ones) come from their dynamic aspects where opportunities emerge in ways which elude control and may even be stymied by it. Indeed, an influential school of thought in strategic management holds that managers overestimate the extent to which they can control events in general and would do better to treat strategy as an emergent process (Mintzberg and Waters, 1985).

An orientation towards understanding the environment and other members' perspectives, clarity about the contribution their organisation is bringing to the network and a gradual, circumspect approach to control emerges as the practical imperatives for a manager intent on reaping the benefits of networking as a route to business growth. One can recognise a similar set of behaviours supporting the career-focused individual networker: active listening, clarity as to what they have to offer (e.g. through the fabled 'elevator pitch'; see Box 4.1) and taking a long-term view of developments rather than attempting to force events through control.

Viewpoint 4.3 What can my organisation do for you?

When I worked for an ad agency I would kind of get on board with the party line and feel like I was representing the agency when I was out and about. So, it was very important to find an agency that, sort of, reflected... me. What I wanted, and that kind of thing. And my agency, you know people referred to it as my spiritual home and all that kind of stuff. So it wasn't just a job, it was more like an organisation I was part of, and contributing towards.

I think I was a naturally good networker in that industry because I had a lot of personality. I was personable. Well-liked, I wasn't, kind of, crazy. I had stuff to say. I was opinionated but I knew how to behave myself, wasn't bad mannered. I was professional. Um, this is professional networking I guess, but I would say that I was an extrovert and so I found it easy and I didn't see it as networking but people would say to me 'oh, you're a brilliant networker'.

The practical importance of understanding your environment makes it useful to have an overall model from which to get your bearings when managing in networks. Covering a range of network types (from incipient to established configurations) Möller and Halinen (2017) offer a model which emphasises sensitivity to context (see Figure 4.1 for a simplified adaptation). Beginning with the 'field', the macro setting for the network, their model highlights the importance of life cycle stage. In a relatively new field such as nanotechnology, the actors involved, the regulatory framework and the pace of change will be quite different

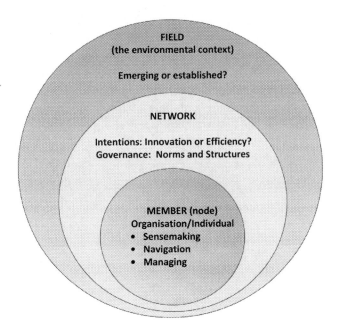

FIGURE 4.1 A model for managing in networks.

from those in an established field of activity such as automotive manufacturing. This is not to underestimate the complexity of the latter, nor the sometimes radical changes that take place in apparently stable industries. But the level of dynamism of the field in which it is embedded can help explain aspects of an individual network, making it more manageable for business growth.

At the specific network level, the key dimensions cover the intentions (goals and value systems) and governance (boundaries, organisation and control mechanisms) of different kinds of networks. The mixture varies from one situation to another, but produces the norms and structures facing a manager in each case. To echo the examples given for the field level, a network oriented towards innovation is likely to be relatively loosely controlled, perhaps with many weak ties and a healthy level of heterogeneity among members (apart from their common orientation to the field). However, a network intending efficiency, a goal typical of networks in established fields, is likely to be more formal and homogeneous in membership. The distinction Burt (1992) makes between loose 'entrepreneurial' networks and denser, more mature 'clique' networks is relevant here. The latter are more focused on exploitation of existing opportunities, the former on exploration of potential ones.

Network activity depends on networkers, so the final level of the framework finds the individual actor characterised by their:

- Role and position
- Available resources and capabilities (including individual skills and experience)
- Goals

Our adaptation of the model places both the individual organisation and the individual within the organisation at this level – both have network roles, resources to share and goals. We are also making the assumption that there will be a high level of goal congruency between most organisations and their members, but this may not always be the case. Ultimately the individual networker's personal interpretation of what is going on will dictate their response to the situation in question.

The framework at Figure 4.1 leads to a list of appropriate management responses to the challenge of networking which complement the orientation towards external understanding, internal focus and circumspect control identified in our earlier discussion of Hakansson and Ford (2002). Möller and Halinen (2017) acknowledge multiple ways of grouping or labelling such responses, but we have simplified them into three headings:

- Sense-making (through sharing ideas and agendas)
- Navigation (helping steer the network)
- Managing (increasing efficiency and effectiveness and network maintenance)

A more generic way of understanding these managerial recommendations is as versions of the familiar strategy formula (e.g. see Reed, 2020) of analysis (listening and understanding), choice (of individual focus and collective navigation) and implementation (through maintenance and nurture of emergent opportunities).

The recommendations also correspond to key elements of the Network-IN model developed through the primary research underpinning this book (see Chapter 1). *Intelligence* emerged as a dominant theme in sense-making activities; *influence* as a dominant theme for navigation (both as collective influence directed externally from the network and as influencing within the network); and *innovation* as both a benefit of networking and, in terms of process innovation, a way of managing network presence. While the format of Table 4.1 implies that these elements are sequential, they overlap and coexist for managers across their networking engagement and in networks of different stages of maturity. For example, process innovation can happen as a result of networking in even well-established industries, simultaneously generating innovation and efficiency.

Viewpoint 4.4 Sense-making and innovation

They are thought leaders, as we call them. They're generating ideas on how payments will look in the future, important issues of compliance within banking like anti-money laundering, know your customer and, and... so on. I'm trying to provide services to these people so I'm interested in knowing what's coming along the pipe. It's collaboration in the context of innovation really; service innovation.

86 Networking for business growth

> My company is quite a small company. We have developed by doing things that bigger companies will be doing in four or five years' time. So, our clients need something for... know your customer now; or they need something for anti-money laundering today. The big companies will come along with something in five years' time. We will develop something today that they can be using. Maybe some of our clients have been using our software for 20 or 30 years, but we'll be developing things more agilely.
>
> So, it means that we need to be at the front. We need to be where those thoughts are happening.

TABLE 4.1 Network management behaviours

Adapted from Hakansson and Ford (2002)	Adapted from Moller and Halinen (2017)	Conventional strategy process model (e.g. Reed, 2020)	Network-IN dominant themes
External understanding and network empathy (listening)	Sense-making (shared)	Analysis	Intelligence
Internal focus (clarity of offer and signalling)	Navigation (helping steer)	Choice	Influence
Circumspect control	Managing (benefits realisation and network maintenance)	Implementation	Innovation

Developing strategic networking capability for business growth

Strategy scholars have long been interested in teasing out what it is about some organisations that makes them successful, in the hope of enhancing and replicating such success. This has led to a school of thought in strategy research known as the Resource-Based View (Barney, 1991). According to this perspective, the key to success for organisations does not lie in chasing market opportunities which may or may not be appropriate to their strengths. Instead, it lies in understanding and cultivating what they are good at (their capabilities) through identifying and combining the resources (intangible, tangible and human) on which such capabilities are based (Grant, 2018). For example, some organisations boast customer service as a capability which gives them an edge over their competitors in key markets. This capability depends on a relevant combination of resources such as excellent training procedures (intangible), access to comprehensive customer data from sophisticated IT equipment (tangible) and highly motivated staff (human).

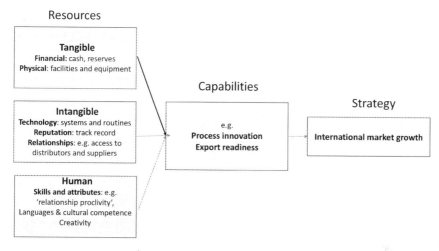

FIGURE 4.2 Resource-based view of strategy.

Gancarczyk and Gancarczyk (2018), researching European Small- or Medium-Sized Enterprises (SMEs), demonstrate that networking helps organisations access resources they lack individually, allowing them to develop important capabilities relevant to areas like international growth. We can illustrate this with a hypothetical example. Figure 4.2 illustrates how a firm hypothetically might be able to execute an international strategy by sourcing the intangible resource of 'access to distributors' from its network rather than from within. This would facilitate its development of export readiness as a capability, enabling its internationalisation strategy. Gancarczyk and Gancarczyk caution against relying on the network for resources which contribute to core capabilities (those that give you a competitive edge) as this can lead to being locked into relationships in a way which creates undue constraints. Our hypothetical firm would therefore do well to develop distributor relationships as a resource on its own account as it grows its international business. This is relevant to managing the paradox of balancing opportunity with constraint, identified earlier in this chapter in the discussion of Hakansson and Ford (2002). Being clear about your core capabilities also bolsters your influence within the network – another characteristic of successful networking covered in that discussion (see also Box 4.1). For example, our imaginary firm in Figure 4.2 also has a capability in process innovation from its human resource of 'creativity' and intangible resource of 'track record', which allows it to influence its network through offering them a reference point for such innovation.

Importantly for our purposes in this book, networking is itself a capability which can give certain organisations a competitive edge. But what kind of resources are necessary to its maintenance and/or development? In a study of Iranian automotive parts firms, Mitrega et al. (2017) have explored this

88   Networking for business growth

question, framing networking as a 'dynamic capability' (Teece, 2007), part of a subset of organisational capabilities which help their possessors thrive in fast-changing environments. They define 'Networking Capability' as 'the complex organizational capability oriented towards managing business relationships along all main relationship life cycle stages' (Mitrega et al., 2017, p. 739). The life cycle stages in question involve finding and attracting the right kind of new partners, working with them effectively as part of a network, and importantly, diagnosing and disengaging from network relationships that have outlived their usefulness.

The necessary resources to support Networking Capability include the intangible one of signalling skills (in order to attract the right kind of partners), the tangible one of robust IT systems (to help evaluate relationships at all stages of the life cycle) and the human one of people who share what Mitrega et al. (2017, p. 585) call 'relationship proclivity' (a willingness to work closely with partners rather than keeping them at arms' length). As we observed earlier in our discussion of Hakansson and Ford (2002), there are clear parallels between managing an organisational network and networking on one's own behalf. This also holds true for Mitrega et al.'s findings. Clarity of communication, a systematic approach to gathering and using information and being prepared to call it a day when mutual opportunities have dried up, are sound principles in both organisational and individual networking contexts.

Viewpoint 4.5 Understanding when it's time to call it a day

I think we've been bought second chances through socialising so I can think of an example of a marketing director who we became... I would say they became quite good friends because we kept socialising, networking with him and his board. I think once or twice he might, we might have got sacked, and we were able to, kind of, get in there and go 'come on hear our point of view', and, you know, we weren't, so that's a kind of positive.

I mean there were people that I definitely grew to like and respect because I'd spent that time with them and I think I definitely began to empathise with their side, the position that they were in. So, you know, if you had a big contract and then a company came to you and they didn't sound really sorry; they just said we are putting this out to pitch and you gotta cut your costs. I could suddenly see that that wasn't personal, that the marketing director had been sat on by the board; that they were in a very difficult position and I could empathise more with the pressures that they were under: and I think I did get to know those people as people too.

Some practical implications: internal networking

Depending on the attitude to networking prevalent in an individual company and your relative level of seniority, you may or may not get the opportunity to be invited to represent your organisation externally at a networking event. This doesn't mean that you cannot hone your networking skills internally, which may in itself lead to you having increased visibility and thus obtaining opportunities to network externally. One way to increase the possibility of this is to refine your 'elevator pitch' so that you can succinctly promote that possibility when the opportunity arises.

BOX 4.1 THE ELEVATOR PITCH

Do a web search for 'elevator pitch' and you will get page after page of hits on how to deliver the perfect persuasive package in the time it takes to travel a few floors with that influential decision maker you just followed into the lift...

Reassuringly, they all say more or less the same thing:

- Understand the kind of opportunity or contact you are seeking (e.g. by working on your listening skills).
- Identify what you can offer uniquely to a network/partner. For an organisation, this could be your core capability, and for an individual it could be a specialist skill not readily available elsewhere.
- Make your pitch as relevant as possible: think brevity, clarity and language. Received wisdom for the elevator pitch is to keep it under 60 seconds (perhaps depending on the speed of the elevator?). For an organisation, this translates into clear, consistent signalling, based on coherent internal focus.
- Aim at mutual benefit in the long term rather than overnight results.

You can see the parallels between how organisations and individual networkers need to analyse their environments, choose the right networks and partners, communicate their unique contributions through clear signalling and not be overly concerned with control.

From the perspective of the organisation, fostering and encouraging effective internal networking is a useful way of strengthening networking competence in employees and developing a shared understanding of how networking is done within that specific organisational culture.

90 Networking for business growth

> ## Viewpoint 4.6 Internal networking
>
> So, I think having the ability to communicate vertically and horizontally and cross pollinate between different groups of individuals who might not have come across each other is something I particularly enjoy actually. Seeing opportunities that might not exist when you only deal in quite linear ways – if you think about cluster or pattern as opposed to a straight line – then you can see how things might intersect quite nicely.

Ritter and Gemunden (2003) in a study of 308 German SMEs found that organisations whose employees network effectively with one another develop better and more profitable external networks (both in terms of improving their position in the networks of which they are part and the related skill of managing their relationships with specific partners). The authors are silent on what proportion of their sample achieved this exacting balance, concentrating instead on proving the statistical correlation between successful external networking and habits of internal networking. They point to the following characteristics as relevant here:

- Network orientation of human resource management systems (recruiting, developing and rewarding employees in a way which encourages internal and external networking)
- Integration of communication structures (which enables clear signalling and a consistent focus on what the organisation or individual can contribute to a network)
- Openness of corporate culture (where sharing of information is seen as the norm)

The successful operation of these factors requires financial, physical, informational and human resources. This demanding combination produces a situation where 'a firm is not only able to intensify its external relations but can also improve its own performance' (p. 751). As well as the technical and economic skills necessary to successful networking, Ritter and Gemunden foreground the 'social qualifications' essential to the effective deployment of such skills. Their list includes 'communication ability, extraversion, conflict management skills, empathy, emotional stability, self-reflectiveness, sense of justice, and cooperativeness' (p. 748).

This is clearly a demanding inventory, cataloguing a rare combination of talents. But note that each of these skills or attributes is located at the level of the individual. Internal networking opportunities facilitate the development of networking competences by each employee, simultaneously creating networking

Networking for business growth **91**

capability at the corporate level. This is an interesting reversal of the view we cited from Luthans (1988) towards the start of this chapter, which suggested a tension between individual networking proclivity and managerial effectiveness. In one sense, it marks a change in how businesses operate or, at least, in their perceptions of how they operate. As we have already observed, the intricate interdependencies within contemporary organisations and business ecosystems means that managers do not have a choice about whether to be involved in networking. The choice is how actively to manage their involvement.

Just as external networking is difficult to get right (Watson, 2007), so internal networking can face significant challenges. Even in relatively non-hierarchical organisations, distrust and lack of mutual understanding between departments creates inefficiencies, hampering external relationships in turn. Schutz and Bloch (2006) diagnosed what they call the 'silo virus' in a study of over 300 German companies, extending their medical analogy into a discussion of the 'broken bones' of organisations caused by a lack of joined-up thinking or planning. They see the cure to this as individual 'bridge builders' prepared to conceive and progress initiatives across departmental and functional boundaries. From the perspective of this chapter, these managers effectively treat their organisations as a network rather than a formal hierarchy, exchanging information and resources with internal contacts in voluntary and relatively informal relationships. With reference to Table 4.1, they use sense-making to manage perceptions of their own department and behaviour in the wider organisation, ensuring the stereotypes beloved of interdepartmental rivalry that give way to a clearer image of reality for all parties. Bridge-builders also demonstrate network navigation, using shared goals to motivate and influence allies in other departments, having carefully managed the choice of such allies in the first place.

Organisations can create the conditions for internal networkers to build bridges by planning in such a way as to ensure that all relevant departments share accountability for the delivery of innovation such as new projects. This establishes any innovation as a joint effort at an early stage rather than, for example, involving users only after work on new IT or finance systems has been initiated by the 'owner' department (whose members may have very different priorities from the rest of the organisation). Most importantly from an internal networking 'seeding' point of view, it forces people to work together on common goals – finding informal as well as formal solutions in a way that builds social capital. On a less strategic level, even something as simple as routine training and development events can provide opportunities for increasing interdepartmental contact and information exchange on an informal basis, as can work shadowing and placement initiatives. While such officially sanctioned measures may appear to run counter to the 'voluntary' nature of networking within a framework of personal reciprocity, they still allow for more spontaneous expressions of collaboration, while confirming the network orientation of human resource management systems endorsed by Ritter and Gemundsen (2003) as a contributor to networking competence.

92 Networking for business growth

Viewpoint 4.7 Developing your elevator pitch via business breakfasts

You go for a breakfast quite early, so you're going to get yourself out of bed, and you have to do a two-minute pitch on what your business is. Which is a really good opportunity to focus and refine your elevator pitch, because you get an immediate reaction. People either understand what it is that you're offering or they don't. Over weeks, you can polish that up until if somebody says 'what do you do?' you've got a natural pitch that you've developed with a group of peers who are all in the same boat. They've all started their own business and so you can learn from them

Conclusion

It is difficult to give a hard and fast answer to the question of how networking affects business growth. Business growth itself depends on so many factors other than networking activity, some of them beyond the control of the individual or organisation. Tangible outcomes from networking relationships can take a long time to come to fruition, making attribution uncertain. For all that, there is significant academic research evidence (e.g. the studies by Ritter and Gemundsen (2003), Watson (2007, 2011), Mitrega et al. (2017) and Gancarczyk and Gancarczyk (2018) cited in this chapter) of a positive relationship between networking activity and business growth and survival in a variety of industries and national cultures. There are caveats (notably from Watson's studies), and sensitivity to context is important because of the wide variety of available network types (Möller and Halinen, 2017); but the overall picture suggests that the new ideas and resources to which networking provides access play a significant role in how businesses move forward into new products, services, processes and markets. Furthermore, the general principles observed by these researchers resonate with those espoused by practitioners, including many of our respondents, about the efficacy of personal networking efforts in creating the conditions for new business as well as sustaining current customers.

Viewpoint 4.8 Slow burn

I have met people who go and if they don't get any sales after the first two or three meetings, they don't go again. You've got to realise that it's not about going into a meeting, giving your card out and getting business there and then, unless you're selling a low value item that you might pick up some business from. But generally, the business you get comes later. One chap I do business with said: 'I don't know if you remember but we met four years ago at a business lunch'. And then we did some business. But that was four years it took. So, it's not a quick and instant thing. To me it's the difference between marketing and sales.

Relationship marketing sees links between suppliers and customers as the essential source of value in marketing systems, especially when seen in the context of wider networks. It provides a useful theoretical framework for understanding how networks add value. Managing one's position in a network to best effect requires steering between opportunity and constraint, influencing and being influenced and the degree of control that can (or should) be exercised within a network. Environmental awareness, clear signalling and taking a long-term perspective are appropriate management responses. These activities can also be understood as sense-making, navigation and managing. The strategic concept of resources and capabilities provides a useful framework for considering how to become more effective at networking. Intangible and tangible resources form the basis for the technical side of networking. Human resources, particularly attitudinal attributes and collaborative skills, are equally important. Together, they underpin networking capability, a form of dynamic capability suited to fast-changing environments.

Internal networking by employees within an organisation make it less prone to 'silo culture' and contribute to the development of competences and attributes which lead to external networking capability.

Networking narratives

4. The power of picking the phone up

I started on a graduate scheme, which meant that straight away I had a group of peers on my cohort who didn't necessarily just work in retail operations. They might work in logistics or purchasing, finance, marketing and so on. So sometimes, I'd go into a new store and there might be a problem, a fundamental issue that people had just accepted, as that's just the way things happened here; and it might be that I've been able to pick the phone up and have a conversation with somebody who's either been able to directly help me themselves or put me in touch with someone else.

The depot, which is just up the road from Birmingham, meant that I was actually able to phone the transport managers and say 'Look I really don't need any more bananas. Just scrap that delivery. Allocate it to someone else, send it to a bigger store that can handle that volume'. You know, 'protect me', essentially, and that would happen from time to time as well.

I think you know, sometimes it could be quite a big, yeah, quite a big fundamental change, or other times it was just a little operational tweak just to help me get through a speed bump on the day. But that's the kind of way I would wield my network. It was very often picking up the phone and having a conversation with somebody

I remember one famous occasion three weeks before Christmas. An 18-wheel truck came packed to the rafters with pallets of PG Tips, which had 100% extra free and had been marked down to 50% off. It was, like, the

94 Networking for business growth

deal of the century for tea bags. One of my contacts had told me about this. I said, 'Yes I'll take everything you've got', and he literally sent me it all on one delivery three weeks before Christmas. So, people were going absolutely nuts about it, but it sold like hot cakes and the customers were incredibly chuffed about it. And then, you know, people… that had started the morning off crying… by the afternoon our sales had gone up by about ten grand on the day, just because of this one big delivery. And that had actually sorted out our wages and our waste, which were a function of our sales. So, by the afternoon everyone's delighted about it.

Every now and then it would, it would provoke a bit of an issue because it came out of left field. It wasn't always that I was being the shrewd operator that I like to think I am. Sometimes I caused myself a few problems along the way!

Ask yourself?

1. What are the risks and the benefits associated with more entrepreneurial forms of networking activity?
2. What kinds of strategic resources are being deployed in this example?
3. How would you assess the internal networking capacity of this organisation, based on what you read here?
4. What advice might you give to the speaker if you were their line manager? Might this be different if you were one of the peers in their network?

References

Bagozzi, R.P. (1974, October) 'Marketing as an Organized Behavioral System of Exchange,' *Journal of Marketing* 38: 77–81, doi: 10.1177/002224297403800414

Barney, J. B. (1991) 'Firm Resources and Sustained Competitive Advantage,' *Journal of Management* 17(1): 99–120, doi: 10.1177/014920639101700108

Burt, R.S. (1992) *Structural Holes*, Cambridge, MA: Harvard University Press.

Burt, R.S. (2004) 'Structural Holes and Good Ideas,' *The American Journal of Sociology* 110(2): 349–399, doi: 10.1086/421787

Forret, M.L. and Dougherty, T.W. (2001) 'Correlates of Networking Behaviour for Managerial and Professional Employees,' *Group & Organization Management* 26: 283–311, https://doi.org/10.1177/1059601101263004

Gancarczyk, M. and Gancarczyk, J. (2018) 'Proactive International Strategies of Cluster SMEs,' *European Management Journal* 36: 59–70, doi: 10.1016/j.emj.2017.03.002

Gibson, C., Hardy, III, J.H. and Buckley, M.R. (2014) 'Understanding the Role of Networking in Organizations,' *The Career Development International* 19: 146–161, doi:10.1108/CDI-09–2013–0111

Grant, R.M. (2018) *Contemporary Strategy Analysis*, 10th ed., New York: John Wiley and Sons [Online]. Available at: https://learning-oreilly-com.libezproxy.open.ac.uk/library/view/contemporary-strategy-analysis/9781119495727/c05.xhtml#head-2-63 (Accessed 10th February 2021).

Gummesson, F. (1995) Relationship Marketing: Its Role in the Service Economy,' in Glynn, W.J. and Barnes, J.G. (eds), *Understanding Services Management*. New York: John Wiley & Sons, pp. 244–268.

Hakansson, H. and Ford, D. (2002) 'How Should Companies Interact in Business Networks?,' *Journal of Business Research* 55(2): 133–139, doi: 10.1016/S0148-2963(00)00148-X

Hollander, S.C., Rassuli, K.M., Jones, D. G. B. and Dix, L.F. (2005) 'Periodization in Marketing History,' *Journal of Macromarketing* 25(1): 32–41, doi: 10.1177/0276146705274982

Kotler, P., Armstrong, G., Harris, L.C. and Piercy, N. (2017) *Principles of Marketing*, 7th European edition, Harlow: Pearson.

Kotter, J. (1982) *The General Managers*, New York: The Free Press.

Luthans, F. (1988) 'Successful Vs. Effective Real Managers,' *The Academy of Management Executive* 2(2): 127, doi: 10.5465/AME.1988.4275524

Luthans, F., Hodgetts, R.M. and Rosenkrantz, S. (1988) *Real Managers*, Cambridge, MA: Ballinger.

Mintzberg, H. and Waters, J.A. (1985) 'Of Strategies, Deliberate and Emergent,' *Strategic Management Journal* 6(3): 257–272, doi: 10.1002/smj.4250060306.

Mitrega, M., Forkmann, S., Zaefarian, G. and Henneberg, S.C. (2017) 'Networking Capability in Supplier Relationships and Its Impact on Product Innovation and Firm Performance,' *International Journal of Operations & Production Management* 37(5): 577–606, doi: 10.1108/IJOPM-11-2014-0517

Möller, K. and Halinen, A. (2017) 'Managing Business and Innovation Networks—From Strategic Nets to Business Fields and Ecosystems,' *Industrial Marketing Management* 67: 5–22, https://doi.org/10.1016/j.indmarman.2017.09.018

Orpen, C. (1996) 'Dependency as a Moderator of the Effects of Networking Behaviour on Managerial Career Success,' *The Journal of Psychology* 130(6): 245–248, doi: 10.1080/00223980.1996.9915006

Porter, M.E. (1985) *Competitive Advantage: Creating and Sustaining Superior Performance*, New York: The Free Press.

Reed, K.B. (2020) *Strategic Management*, Virginia Tech Publishing via Open Textbook Library [Online]. Available at https://open.umn.edu/opentextbooks/textbooks/73 (Accessed 29th January 2021).

Ritter, T. and Gemunden, H.G. (2003) 'Network Competence: Its Impact on Innovation Success and Its Antecedents,' *Journal of Business Research* 59(9): 745–755, doi: 10.1016/S0148-2963(01)00259-4

Schütz, P. and Bloch, B. (2006) 'The "Silo-Virus": Diagnosing and Curing Departmental Groupthink,' *Team Performance Management* 12(1/2): 31–43, doi: 10.1108/13527590610652783

Teece, D.J. (2007) 'Explicating Dynamic Capabilities: The Nature and Microfoundations of (Sustainable) Enterprise Performance,' *Strategic Management Journal* 28(13): 1319–1350, doi: 10.1002/smj.640

Watson, J. (2007) 'Modeling the Relationship between Networking and Firm Performance,' *Journal of Business Venturing* 22(6): 852–874, doi: 10.1016/j.jbusvent.2006.08.001

Watson, J. (2011) 'Networking: Gender Differences and the Association with Firm Performance,' *International Small Business Journal* 30(5): 536–558, doi: 10.1177/026624261038488

Wolff, H.G. and Moser, K. (2009) 'Effects of Networking on Career Success: A Longitudinal Study,' *Journal of Applied Psychology* 94(1): 196–206, doi: 10.1037/a0013350

5

NETWORKING FOR SOCIAL CHANGE

Introduction

The history of humanity has been characterised by transformation and change, often driven by industrial and technological development, but just as often resulting from social movements driven by cultural and philosophical considerations. These latter considerations, which might find an origin through a counterculture of resistance to the dominant ideas of the time, may be articulated and made visible through art, literature or critical debate. In time, as they find their way into mainstream thinking, they influence all aspects of society until they become the dominant ideology, which is itself undermined by the next big wave of ideas.

What concerns us in the chapter is the role that networking may play in the spread of social transformation and cultural change. In particular, we will look at the ways that digital networking has the potential to speed up social innovation and the ways too that resistance to social change can be marshalled through online fora. In Chapter 2, we considered the ethical implications of networking and, in particular, concerns that may arise for less powerful participants. The discussion there is particularly relevant to this present chapter.

This kind of change can be viewed as 'social innovation', defined by Cajaiba-Santana (2014) as the 'creation of a greater common good'. As we discussed in Chapter 1, networking is an essential way in which new ideas, activities and technologies can be developed, and this is as true of social change as business or economic development.

Moral identity and idealism in networking

The questionnaire research carried out in preparation of this book shows that a strong motivation for networking is a wish to 'give back' in some way to the community or communities, which have given to an individual opportunity

DOI: 10.4324/9781003026549-6

Networking for social change **97**

or perhaps opened doors for them. Collaborative motivations such as sharing common experiences (61%) and developing shared approaches (37%) were more commonly indicated than explicitly competitive ones such as finding out about competitors (20%) and stealing ideas (10%). One in four indicated mentoring junior colleagues as a reason for networking.

At its simplest, this is most usually expressed through professional or occupational networks in which older members of the community transmit their learning to newer members or provide enhanced access to progression. Conversely, some such individuals seek mutual reinforcement through networking with people like themselves, often where they feel the need for reinforcement against structures (such as their workplace) where they feel marginalised, overlooked or degraded.

In the model derived from our research, we call this IN-sight and our definition is repeated here:

> Insight: the outcome sought is to reinforce the ideas or ideals that an individual already holds, for mutual support; or, by mixing with like-minded others, in order to strengthen and confirm their current world view. Through networking activity, the individual is helped to deepen, shape and better align beliefs, attitudes and behaviours. This is sometimes a defensive strategy for peers who share common pressures and who can thus support and maintain a collective sanity in an otherwise chaotic universe. In that way, networking can support a culture of resistance to an unacceptable dominant ideology.

BOX 5.1 PARTICIPATION IN THE AIDS MOVEMENT

Eighty gay and bisexual men and transgender women were recruited into a study in the US, which wanted to find out why they became active in the AIDS movement. What was meant by activism was broadly construed and would encompass activity of the kind we are discussing in this book as 'networking'. Participants came from Chicago and San Francisco, and their ethnicity in the main was Mexican or Puerto Rican.

Researchers interviewed them to discover their life stories and what had brought them to become actively involved in the AIDS movement through a number of different organisations. As in our own research, they found it was common for people to have more than one reason for involvement. In their different ways, participants discussed getting involved to counter what they considered oppressing forces: using activism to 'create and reproduce identity and community through their involvement'.

The researchers identified 11 interconnected reasons for participation:

- Values
- Helping others

98 Networking for social change

- Reciprocity
- Understanding
- Personal development
- Career enhancement
- Community concern
- Social change
- Esteem enhancement
- Personal experience
- Social networking (meeting people like themselves, possibly to have a relationship)

(Adapted from Kuhns and Ramirez-Valles, 2016).

Equally too, as people grow in confidence in their own lives, they start to see opportunities to add value to the communities to which they belong (see Box 5.1). Perhaps after a period of personal networking with others like themselves, the individual actors start to think about how they can raise their voices collectively to try to improve things for others or, more cautiously, for people coming after them. In our model, we refer to networking of this type as IN-fluence:

> Influence: for some people, the primary purpose of networking is to join forces with others in a similar position in order to develop a stronger collective voice with others outside the network, or to lobby for some kind of change to the mutual benefit of their fellow network members.

This takes us back to the discussion in Chapter 1 on 'like/unlike' forms of networking, as people may choose to work with a group with which they identify or, alternatively, to support a group that they see as comparatively disadvantaged in relation to themselves.

Viewpoint 5.1 Inclusivity in local community action networks

There are a lot of people who want to be involved but don't like to use Zoom. They don't like to use technology, so there's a danger that those networks begin to weaken. But hopefully next year they will be resurrected. In communities, there are lots of networks. The difficulty is we are an ageing community: but also, on top of that, the people have time to participate in these networks are old gits like me. Younger people have to go to work. They've got children, they don't – it's not so easy for them; so you tend to get a bias in the network which is perhaps more conservative than it needs to be.

Networking for social change **99**

The rise in digital technologies has vastly increased the ability of individuals to use their personal beliefs and moral identity to impact on wider society. At its simplest, we see this in the force of social movements such as 'Me Too' and 'Black Lives Matter' where the sheer numbers of people voicing support for those suffering discrimination is a part of bringing about overdue change which decades of legislation have failed to enforce. Bhatti et al. (2020) discuss two ways in which this can happen:

1. Promotive voice – the sharing of new ideas to improve the status quo
2. Prohibitive voice – sharing concerns about issues and/or practices that could harm society

Clearly, any individual can do both – voicing positive strategies and using things like hashtags to amplify issues that are important to them while calling out bad behaviours they see in their networks and communities. Bhatti et al. (2020, p. 2) explore the extent to which particular personalities may feel called to use social networking in this kind of way, discussing a 'felt obligation for constructive challenge', which enables a person to behave in ways consistent with their deepest sense of self, and thus make an extra effort to bring about change:

> …social media has provided an outlet for individuals where they can become agents of change by benefitting from the access social media has provided to reach a huge number of users, sometimes even on a global scale.
>
> *(Bhatti et al., 2020, p. 10)*

Viewpoint 5.2 Reasons for engaging

I feel like civic engagement is important. I feel like participating, civic engagement, participation in society, is important. It feels like that's part of, you know, my family values. So, it's acting on that, I guess, finding networks that can plug you in. Living your values is important. We all know that people would like to feel connected. So, I guess there's a sense of that. But there's also the sense of… agency and, your contribution counts, into a bigger social …People want to become more actively involved, to exercise some influence; but, for me personally, I wanted to create a world that is the one I want to exist in and bring my children up in.

Munzel et al. (2018) explored why and how individuals participate in social networks, discovering two different reasons:

1. Social enhancement – to maintain or increase high levels of well-being
2. Social compensation – to compensate themselves for a perceived lack of well-being.

100 Networking for social change

They concluded that well-being is both a driver for and an outcome of such participation. Bhatti et al. (2020) would explain this as relating to self-consistency theory, which suggests that individuals are motivated to indulge in behaviours consistent with their overall self-views, so that they can maintain a cognitive consistency between their attitudes and behaviours. Later in the chapter, we suggest that reciprocity too is an important factor in motivating individuals to follow through their personal beliefs into supporting, advocating for and participating in social change networks. While social networking in support of positive change may reinforce moral identity and thus enhance well-being, it also can lead into an intention to become an active part of a movement for change, resulting in personal change and growth at an individual level.

Wicked problems

One of the singular advantages of networking activity is how it can bring together individuals from very disparate backgrounds, who collectively can do more than any can do individually. Through pooling both collective resources and knowledge derived from very different fields and epistemologies, it is possible to innovate to find new ways of working with intractable problems. In Chapter 3, we considered formal networks, mandated for reasons of public policy. These kinds of networks often use innovation to find new approaches or perspectives on wicked problems. Being mandated, such networks will to some extent have a predetermined mission and possibly objectives. This chapter is concerned with self-mandated very informal networks. Here, we are talking more about individuals who decide for themselves to take some form of collective action. We would contend that networking, in contradistinction to more traditional economic or organisationally based activities, is far more effective in dealing with what are often termed 'wicked problems'.

A wicked problem is a complex problem, one with multiple different ways of framing the issue to be dealt with, dependent on perspective (Rittel and Webber, 1973, Davies, 2016). Equally, identified solutions to a wicked problem have a high probability of unintended consequences that may create further complex needs. The roots of a wicked problem are deep and long term, embedded in the systems that spawn such problems, and requiring the actions of many agents and institutions to address them. For this reason, we argue that networking is the strongest and possibly the only way to build long-term answers to such issues:

> In complexity theory, turbulence is a productive force. Simple perturbations can nudge a system into creative activity. To break up rigidities in conflict and inequity, turbulence is needed, to spark creativity and a new landscape.
>
> *(Davies, 2016, p. 41)*

Networking for social change **101**

As networks work across traditional boundaries and involve all sorts of different actors, they have the capacity to be generative of new ideas. That in itself is insufficient to generate change. For change to happen, the networks need to be capable of positive action, to be able to mobilise individuals and harness community resources and to engage and persuade civic and corporate institutions to work with them.

In understanding why networks have a particular advantage in doing this, it is useful to return to an idea, first raised in Chapter 1, of reciprocity. A singular power of networking is the benefits it bestows on all who are taking part in networking activity, the idea that everyone gains something.

Viewpoint 5.3 The framework of reciprocity

I was a chair of a local charity ... there's also being in the same marketplaces, as it were, where you are trying to achieve many of the same things as other people in the same sector. I guess there is probably a slight amount of competition but generally it's more co-operative in nature and so the networking works well. I've had experiences that other people haven't had, in that I can help them with issues that they're addressing... addressing, and also I find that it helps me with issues I have. Especially if I'm at meetings under Chatham House rules where you can discuss freely. There are things that I can't bounce off colleagues that are easier to bounce off my peers from other organisations. It's sort of like self-mentoring if you like. You are sharing ideas and best practice: and what worked, what didn't work and also getting a feeling of the zeitgeist

The idea of reciprocity was examined by Minas et al. (2019), who identified a progressive four-stage framework of reciprocity in programmes of social change. Their work examined 15 programmes in nine countries, so has the advantage of examining practice in different cultural contexts. The idea that reciprocity grows and develops is useful in particular to thinking about how networking can help to address wicked problems – we are reminded that deep change may often be incremental and slow moving.

Their framework (Minas et al., 2019) shows how programmes can progress from a position that asks 'how can I help these people' to 'how can we work together in the promotion of our collective cause?'; this latter being a position of full reciprocity.

Stage 1: Safety net programmes, supporting people who are struggling with basic resources.
Stage 2: Promotion programmes, which aim to develop strengths, skills and goals. Here, the professionals who are supporting the programme may, to a greater or lesser degree, also develop strengths and skills.

102 Networking for social change

Stage 3: Co-construction programmes, which are mutual development of participants and professionals, enhancing leadership and participation for all.

Stage 4: Social transformation programmes, which fully engage professionals and participants in ways that impact on wider social structures, leading to longer-lasting and more significant social, cultural and economic change.

One useful aspect of the framework (Minas et al., 2019) is the idea that one stage can lead to another. Given the complexity of wicked problems, it might well be that the only place to begin is by alleviating the immediate burden felt by those most impacted by the issue. This can be a useful starting point in a journey that can end with something far bigger. At the same time, Minas et al. (2019) discuss other progressions: a move from formal programmes to far larger and much more informal groups (that we would call networks); a growth in the ambition of goals set; an increasing balancing of power across all those involved; and an increase in community ownership and full participation in the objectives and implementation of the programmes. All these are ideas that will be examined further in this chapter.

Creation of community

Through both the search for identity and a wish to be involved in solving wicked problems, people come into networks based around a shared need, problem or opportunity for social improvement. In terms of reciprocity, a strengthening of an individual within a specific identified community is a clear benefit of this particular type of networking.

At its most simple, networks (whether face to face or online) can support individuals at times of personal challenge. They thus act as a self-help group (see Box 5.2).

BOX 5.2 SHARE, LIKE AND ACHIEVE

A study examined how people used Facebook to support them in reaching their health-related weight loss goals. The network of supporters did not necessarily have to do much to add considerable value to the person asking for their support. This study shows the power of an informal self-help network, which can either be set up by individuals or supported through a formal programme or app. Help consisted of:

- The power of a like
- The strength of a comment
- Going viral by a share
- Support from both strong and weak ties
- Committing to reach a goal
- Asking for help when struggling

> Support in such sensitive situations, can come from weak ties while on-line (casual acquaintances and online friends). Such weak ties provide different viewpoints, objective feedback, reduced risks and reduced role obligations without evoking the social apprehensiveness that might come from attempting to share emotions in face-to-face interactions.
>
> *(p. 497)*
>
> *(Adapted from De La Pena and Quintanilla, 2015)*

In some cases, this may lead to more practical offers of support or joint supportive action such as individuals coming together to fundraise for a particular goal which will help their group manage better. Perhaps at this stage they might be joined by a range of other supporters – close connections of those who need help or people around who are interested in the cause.

Sinapuelas and Foo (2019) suggest four different ways that networks might support their members:

- Education and awareness raising
- Personal support
- Prevalence monitoring (reporting on the extent of the problem)
- Two-way channel of communication

They report that the ways actors will participate in such support networks are contingent on both their level of trust in the network and their social connections to it:

> we find trust playing a significant role in information getting… Our results identify one factor that encourages information giving. We find individuals with social connections are more likely to give information. Moral obligations to their social connections may compel individuals to act in a socially desirable manner by sharing health information and contributing to the shared knowledge base. Absent these social connections, individuals may act in self-interest and focus on getting information.
>
> *(Sinapuelas and Foo, 2019, p. 699)*

The next stage of network formation comes when such groups start to set themselves longer-term goals, perhaps moving away from immediate support for named individuals to fighting for the cause more generally. This can include a political set of actions, such as lobbying for a change in legislation. At all stages, a sense of community is built around those involved, whether formally or informally.

Viewpoint 5.4 Community and mobilisation

I think the anti-racism work flipped a switch in my mind linguistically. I would have said I was always 'not racist' but I didn't do anything to be actively anti-racist and that's influenced a lot of how I view other things I feel passionately about. I care about the climate and climate change, but what was I actually doing? So, plugging into a network that's doing the work, and you can just do your bits in it and come in and out. It's a useful resource and tool, so technology... social networks, when used appropriately, are you know... a complete lifeblood, power behind some of these movements: but obviously they work in the same way for opposing movements.

And I felt like I was making my contribution and then when I saw some of those networks and individuals be thanked publicly for their work by Joe Biden, I felt really proud of them and I felt... I felt part of that too.

It was nice to feel part of the collective who were all working towards a common purpose and a common goal that I believed in and wanted to be part of implementing.

In larger movements, all three of these types of networking activities (self-help, practical support and lobbying) can come together, leading to what Maxey et al. (2015, p. 432) describe as 'radical civic transitions'. They give a number of examples where locally based networks are effective at mobilising, connecting and coordinating collective resources towards a desired social innovation. While such groups may start in opposition to the established structures locally, which are rooted in place and have both legitimacy and power, in reality they work with those structures to co-create the civic institutions of the future. The strength of the radical movements is that they are fine-grained and bottom-up agents of social change.

One example discussed by Maxey et al. (2015) is of local groups of would-be residents who wished to establish settlements that can support sustainable lifestyles and livelihoods, often for people priced out of a commercially driven local property market. In reality, these groups will have to work with planners to fulfil their aspirations. Equally, planners are subject to their own performance outcomes designed to meet local, national and international aspirations for sustainable development. While there is the possibility to build bridges, Maxey et al. (2015) report that such resident-led groups are nine times more likely to form and then fold than to realise their goals. The value of wider networks of supporters, including those who have done such work elsewhere, is to share lessons and help make the social and economic case needed by planning authorities. So, such networks, while offering radical alternatives to the status quo, in reality are boundary spanning and inherently collaborative, brokering constructive challenge while advocating fundamental change. In that sense, they need to be viewed as transformative, not reformist: working for a reimagined civic geography, but through co-design and co-creation. There are positive examples of this working in practice, but also many examples that illustrate how hard it is to challenge established ways of working (Box 5.3).

BOX 5.3 REGENERATION DREAM FADES

A serious attempt was made by Dutch citizens to set up community enterprises (CEs) to provide services in disadvantaged communities. As had worked successfully internationally, the idea was to empower local people to fill gaps in provision that had resulted from austerity cuts. A three-year study showed slow progress and many obstacles, revealing a significant gap between the positive intentions of those involved and the realisation of outcomes. Although participants attempted to adapt ideas for the local context, cultural resistances still prevented progress. Among the problems identified were risk aversion, a lack of trust and concerns around accountability:

> In the context of a Dutch policy discourse that strongly favours active citizenship, "do-it-yourself" democracy and entrepreneurship, this article has revealed a large discrepancy between professionals' positive attitudes towards community enterprise start-ups and institutional responses. While local professionals comply with the self-organization discourse, their accounts reveal ambivalent and contradictory responses of their organizations, supporting and simultaneously resisting "disruptive" entrepreneurial actions from citizens, despite efforts from boundary spanners to prevent or mitigate this resistance. Instead of (steps towards) co-production, institutional responses often turn out as forms of "counter-production" that keep community enterprises (CEs) in full uncertainty and dependence about the acquisition of assets, crucial information or (legal) consent for various activities, sometimes smothering the motivation of CE initiators. As such, institutional responses have damaged the trust that was initially built by positive interactions with CE initiators... Hence, the positive attitudes of local professionals regularly convey false promises regarding the actual willingness of their institutions to co-produce services and benefits with CEs.

> *(p. 1513)*

> *(Adapted from Kleinhans, 2017)*

Whose voice is loudest?

Where a wider network coalesces around a smaller group in order to support them, such as the residents discussed above, there is a danger that local voices can be drowned out by others who are more confident by virtue of having already

106 Networking for social change

lived through such transformative change, or by professionals who come to support, but end by silencing. This is a problem identified in many attempts to involve local people in transformative change – it needs to be about more than just 'having their say'. True involvement is about having a voice and being actively involved across all activities in the network.

Viewpoint 5.5 Voices in the neighbourhood

I've had some quite forthright views expressed, which is good. In a meeting, I've been described as...certain things. Debate works but it's not...when things can become contentious the public meeting falls apart because it becomes not a democratic process but a slanging match. The people with the loudest voices will carry it. But every community will face the same thing.

You'll never move the extremes one way or the other. The only people you can move are the ones who are in the middle, who will vary from the 'I support this with caveats' to 'I don't support it but I would support it, if this'. But somebody who is blinkered – because, was it Jonathan Swift who said: 'you can't reason a person out of an opinion that they were never reasoned into in the first place'? Their reasons are not rational.

Critical hospitality theorists Cockburn-Wootten et al. (2018) confronted this issue when they worked with local people to make the goals of tourism relevant and embedded in local communities, not just seen as an economic endeavour. Their response is to recommend the principles of dialogue theory, which is 'defined as inductive processes that negotiate power and establish channels of communication for outcomes to happen' (Cockburn-Wootten et al., 2018, p. 1487).

There are three parts to this:

1. Generative – 'risking one's position in order to arrive at new understandings, and a commitment to keeping the conversation going' (Zoller, 2000, p. 193)
2. Diversity – an appreciation of difference, both between individual actors and between different constituent groups
3. Power – equalised, with no attempt to persuade or achieve specific outcomes

The need to hear different voices and not to privilege one kind of response over another can present specific issues when the time comes to disseminate the outcomes of the dialogue. For networks who play a key role in brokering agreement with establishment bodies, dissemination activity may well be presented in forms acceptable to the receiver, for example, through a written report or perhaps a formal presentation to a committee. Presenting an intellectually coherent case and summarising the dialogue in ways that make a case easy for the listener to assimilate can mean that conversations are tidied up and minority positions omitted. Thus, individuals may feel their ideas have been appropriated or their voices silenced.

One route forward is to create peer-led networks, which have sometimes been described as 'participatory democracies'. Though not without their challenges, the benefits of taking this approach have been reported as (a) negotiating relationships, (b) feeling the responsibility of involvement and (c) sharing power (Budge et al., 2019). A similar set of findings from the US report that:

> The perceived challenges included a lack of clear goals and measurements of success, an absence of leadership and direction, and a shortage of resources. The successes included passion of partners, increased collaboration, and increasing and maintaining social capital within the community.
>
> *(Strauss et al., 2019, p. 402)*

In a peer-led process, participants choose how the network will work, how activities are carried out and who will assume leadership at different stages and for different processes. While this kind of decision-making may seem slower, it is not necessarily the case if later difficulties and disagreements are anticipated and resolved through full participation. At the same time, it is important to remain aware that giving a full and equal voice to all will not necessarily change organisational processes or outcomes in the network – what is changed is the sense of full ownership across all members. It may well be that leadership is given to the 'professional' members of the network, even where such individuals would prefer it to rest with the identified beneficiaries of the network activities.

Viewpoint 5.6 Working with as well as for people

Obviously, people aren't all the same. But... just letting people be conscious of the coping strategies they have and what might have triggered those coping strategies. And the fact that, too often, people in less powerful places fight amongst each other about their different coping strategies rather than working together to challenge the very fact that they need to have coping strategies at all.

Watson and Fox (2018) discussed their wish to devise radical new ways to work with young people, only to find the young participants were happy to adopt traditional methods and to cede power to the professionals. However, the study participants were presented with genuine choices about taking ownership and proposing alternative strategies. The transferable lesson here to participatory networks or to networks with very diverse members is to ensure there is genuine choice. The question must always be asked: how genuine is the wish of the 'professionals' in the network to offer choice or to allow diversity in the voices that are heard?

108 Networking for social change

Often, the intention is there, but the professionals concerned may be removed from a geographically dispersed community or may not have the mechanisms to evaluate how well their work is being received in the network they are supporting.

> It is problematic to assume that young people do not have a voice until adults provide them with one, as various organizational projects seem to claim. The position that young people need to be given a voice by adults neglects young people's on-going contributions to social and political life... Young people have ways of speaking out and speaking up, but these may not register among adults as recognizable or legitimate.
>
> *(Caron et al., 2017, p. 50)*

This knotty problem of how best to deliver the right kind of change in ways which help those who need the help – when such people may be invisible, marginalised or lacking a voice – has concerned theorists for many years. Harold Linstone analysed this problem initially in 1969, and identified four reasons why social change is so difficult. At that time, there was not the same interest in networking as there is currently, but the 2016 reprint of his seminal article shows how relevant his discussion remains.

He identifies four problem areas in developing policy:

1. Long-range objectives are frequently unsuitable – They may be too vague; environments and values are in a state of flux; and there remains a need to develop a series of potential alternative futures that can be debated and discussed rather than to plump too soon for 'the solution'.
2. The 'system' is inadequately understood – It is important to recognise that policymakers don't really understand community action, and vice versa.
3. There is poor meshing of objectives, environment and needs – Here he cites the narrowness of expert thinking, and a modern commentator would add a lack of pluralism and diversity, and insufficient recognition of the impact of change.
4. Fear of the unknown and human inertia – The kinds of problems identified above in Box 5.3.

Linstone (1969) suggests that among the ways forward is for policymakers to gain greater insight, possibly by being embedded in the local context or by employing people from the locality in the organisations which need to change. This points the way to the solution that we would advance – to involve the communities concerned dynamically, in empowered networks that are given a voice that is heard by the powerful and to fully involve these networks in the design and implementation of change, including long-term evaluation and evolution. Only through doing this can different questions be asked, different alternative futures be designed and better futures constructed for the longer-term benefit of all. Wicked problems may never be fully addressed. It is well worth returning to Linstone (1969) to keep a clear focus on how hard it is to find even partial ways of dealing with them.

Social innovation as a driver of social change

The ideas that emerge from the discussion above, to some extent, position individuals against the group consensus in certain kinds of networks, particularly those concerned with transformative change for disadvantaged groups. At a conceptual level, this concerns the relationship between agentic and structuralist frameworks in network theory. As we have discussed in Chapter 1, this may in part be because it is easy to develop theory at the level of the whole network rather than to consider the possibly large numbers of individuals who compromise the network. It may however prove to be particularly difficult when it comes to considering the silencing or marginalising of the very individuals that the network is trying to help. Where the group is working with external institutions to operationalise change, then compromises may result which threaten the autonomy and aspirations of individual agents. Such institutions (the structures of society) may want to work genuinely and with empathy with their ultimate end users (the individual agents), but may lack the cultural competence to bridge gaps in terms of language, pluralism and expectations (Box 5.4):

> A new challenge has appeared in recent times, though: creating alternative future options for those organizations through the active participation of the people involved in – or affected by – them. Despite the obvious and valuable contribution of futures research when it comes to assessing decision-making processes in history, we believe that a gap may appear sometimes between those organizational managers who make projections about the future and the people affected by them when the latter – called "users" here – are not actively involved in those projections. At times the gap is so large that it seriously affects the stability of the organizations themselves, and consequently their own future. Anyway, a lack of empathy with users' expectations would always result in lack of competitiveness for the organizations in question.
>
> *(Bas and Guillo, 2015, p. 287)*

BOX 5.4 HOLDING TO ACCOUNT

There are many significant and documented examples of large corporates being held to account by activists who object to their products or behaviours. Some examples include tobacco companies, the inappropriate use of infant formula in countries with underdeveloped public health systems, sweatshops in the Global South producing clothes for the richer north and fracking in areas of natural beauty. One particular subset of these forms of resistance comes from networks that grow up around a particular illness, which target companies they consider to be the cause of the illness or which are involved in its treatment in ways the network considers unfair.

> Those who mount such challenges will be considered by the management and shareholders of the corporate body as outsiders or even fanatics. But the opposing network may well include professional staff from government agencies or other public bodies as well as individuals who are directly impacted by the company.
>
> The value of such activist networks is that they set an agenda for wider change and may prefigure public policy. They can attract media attention to the cause, especially where they call out hypocritical behaviour or the exploitation of the powerless in the interest of corporate profit.
>
> Such networks may be small and action orientated, focusing on relatively narrow goals for change. But their value is potentially far wider, as different groups with different concerns may have overlapping interests with wider groups. They thus create space for wider social change:
>
> > Networking allows groups to shift the ground of contention and link with wider movements.
>
> *(p. 224)*
>
> *(Adapted from Zoller, 2017)*

The interplay between individuals' agency and the structures surrounding them is discussed by Cajaiba-Santana (2014) specifically in relation to social innovation. As he observes, the literature on social innovation is fragmented and largely reliant on observational case studies. As such, the agency/structure problem is often observed or reported, but remains critically unexamined. His proposed solution is to move from an oppositional relationship between agentic and structural forces in social innovation to a new way of looking at them which sees them as working differently yet collaboratively. 'Agentic' he defines as created through the actions taken by specific individuals and 'structuralist' as determined by the external structural context, usually established institutions. His framework proposes that we see social innovation as arising when collective action and structural contexts co-evolve in the process of creation. This is perhaps an extension of what Bas and Guillo (2015) discuss as 'participatory foresight', based on empathy and a human-centred approach to social innovation.

We would extend this way of seeing the process: involving networking as the key activity which supports the creation of social innovation. As we have seen above, it requires many actors to co-design and co-develop radical change. Usefully though, Cajaiba-Santana reminds us:

> The social innovation process requires attention to the individual persons; more specifically, to what they think, to what they value, to how they behave, and to how inter-relations between actors and social systems take place.
>
> *(Cajaiba-Santana, 2014, p. 48)*

The examples discussed above tend to relate to networks built with smaller communities in mind, working towards a specific social change in a given geographical space. The problems discussed however are just as relevant, and possibly far harder to manage, when the network of beneficiaries of the innovation are connected digitally. Flick et al. (2020) look forward to the potential and identify the pitfalls of using Information and Communication Technology (ICT) to connect to older people, discussing a variety of social and care technologies. Their research identifies a range of ethical issues of the type we are thinking about in this chapter:

- Stereotyping older people
- The human face of ICT
- Privacy and informed consent
- Autonomy
- Anxiety around the technology being used

In response, they anticipate a range of solutions: increased regulation, a corporate shift towards social responsibility and a greater sense of accountability being required by the public of those who manage the network platforms. They discuss the problem of the 'fictional user' – an idealised imaginary member of the online network whose identity is imagined by younger developers of the technologies. And, as we have seen above, their solution is towards co-design and co-production:

> Innovators would benefit from involving older users and creating open communication channels with them.
>
> *(Flick et al., 2020, p. 8)*

Implications for practice

This chapter has raised some difficult questions about the ways in which networks can both support individuals and lead to wider long-term change, and the related problem of 'taking over' and thus increasing the marginalisation of already vulnerable groups. It is not our intention to discourage anyone from either seeking help and support through networking activity or holding back from offering their services through participating in such networks.

It therefore follows that the first practical implication for anyone who is involved in supporting, lobbying or acting in such networks is to consider how their involvement may sustain or reduce inequality or power imbalances. This challenge is usefully considered by Frazer and Watt (2016), when they examined the experiences of older volunteers on a house building project in the Philippines, organised through Rotary International networks. They discuss the phenomenon of 'vicarious trauma', witnessing the pain of others. Their findings are ambivalent, reminding us that such empathic pain can lead to a belief that the volunteers are being offered redemption for their relative privilege through their

112 Networking for social change

> ## Viewpoint 5.7 Serving others
>
> I find myself, if I step outside myself and observe my own behaviour, I find myself being more altruistic. That means thinking less about my own benefits but thinking, how can I help that person to achieve something, even if it comes at some cost to myself.
>
> Now that willingness to bear extra cost is somewhat less powerful when you have networks where the emotional ties are weaker; then I look, maybe even subconsciously perhaps, so 'what do I get out of it if I help that person now?' Whereas with the strong emotional networks 'what do I get out' I think because I like, there is this concept of love like, whatever; that person, I want them to prosper, to make their life somewhat more comfortable, and I don't necessarily immediately think about my rewards although those rewards are intangible; they make me feel good if I've helped somebody and that kind of stuff.

volunteering work, or that the volunteers may construct a narrative of 'poor but happy' which, by romanticising poverty, excuses and perpetuates structural inequity. At the same time, Frazer and Watt describe an 'ethic of hope' that was generative of personal and social change, where volunteers were energised into setting themselves attainable goals and actions:

> Chance encounters with marginalised people surfaced feelings of empathic pain, evoking an affective and emotional politics of hope for things to be otherwise. For one participant in particular, group leader Alan, the subsequent embodied sense of hope impelled him to act. This empathic response to another's unknowable pain presented an urgent ethical challenge he was determined to solve. For Alan, the politically transformative potential of empathy was realised; pain was not mobilised within neoliberal discourses of self-improvement.
>
> *(Frazer and Watt, 2016, p. 187)*

For those who are thinking of joining a network with an altruistic purpose or who are seeking (as many of our research respondents were) to 'give something back' at a particular point in your life, we suggest that you use our six-point SOC-ACT checklist to help you think through what it is that you are looking for (Table 5.1):

Once you have formulated answers to each of these points, you will be in a better position to approach the network or networks that your research throws up. You should expect some kind of a sifting process if you are planning a substantial commitment, resulting in a number of probing questions about your motivation for getting involved. The SOC-ACT checklist will help you with the selection process.

Networking for social change **113**

TABLE 5.1 The SOC–ACT checklist

Area of focus: the network	*Research questions*
Credibility	Who are they – are they reputable? What is their public profile like? Do you know any members? How professional is their website, or any other tools they have for member communications? What have they achieved so far and what are their goals?
Contribution	What are they looking for in you? What outcomes and deliverables are expected? How will you know when your work is done? Will you have any agreement in writing with them, no matter how informal?
Collateral	What support can you expect? What resources do they have? Who will you work with? What community assets or resources can you draw on?
Area of focus: yourself	
Commitment	How strongly do you feel about the mission? How much time will you commit? How much pain will you be willing to go through? Are there any things that might interfere with your commitment?
Conflicts of Interest	Are there any professional barriers to involvement? Have you any personal experience that might help or might get in the way? Who in your life might object to your involvement? Are there aspects of the ways they operate which would embarrass or disturb you such as direct action? What would the neighbours think?
Consequences	What do you want to get out of this? What challenges do you think might shake your world view? How will this strengthen your relationship with your community, your self-identity, your moral values? What do you hope to learn?

There are many different ways to network for social change. As we have seen above, your contribution can be as small as making a positive contribution to social networking in support of your chosen cause. You may want to support network governance by joining a board, or you may want to spend a couple of hours at the weekend in some kind of direct action.

FIGURE 5.1 A simplified version of the social change model applied to networking.

Given the theoretical perspectives discussed above, readers may be asking themselves how best to manage the ethical issues that may be thrown up through networking in a very diverse group, possibly working alongside people from very different backgrounds to your own. Here, the social change model – which looks at the relationship between self/group/community – may prove helpful on a day-to-day basis (Figure 5.1).

There are a number of different versions of this model around, and they can easily be found through the usual search engines. The original is attributed to versions developed in the mid-1990s by The Higher Education Research Institute of University of California, Los Angeles. Their 'Social Change Model of Leadership Development' (HERI, 1996) offers seven attributes to measure in yourself:

1. Consciousness of self – Being aware of one's own values, attitudes and beliefs (and, we would add, also working to recognise and overcome unconscious bias)
2. Congruence – Checking that your behaviours are in line with your values and beliefs
3. Commitment – Utilising the energy which motivates you to serve
4. Collaboration – Examining how well you work with others
5. Common purpose – Ensuring you share a common vision in your network and that all are included in active participation
6. Controversy with civility – Being open to different ideas and views and listening with respect
7. Citizenship – Making sure that your work is leading to positive change on behalf of others and the community

It can be helpful to share models like this across the network, so others can determine with you how this can be operationalised and evidenced in practice. The goal is not just to live one's own individual values but to incorporate group values in all the relationships within and outside the network.

Conclusion

This chapter has considered how an individual actor may start to work with others who share a common outlook. We suggest that over time, there may be

Networking for social change   **115**

a movement from offering one another reciprocal support, help and advice to a recognition that the issue is bigger than the problems or interests of just those at present in the network. At this point, a network may start to work on a larger scale, involving more people either as individuals or through network coalitions, aiming towards some deeper social change or innovation. This development risks excluding those very people who are intended to benefit from the innovation. On a personal level and collectively, members of the network need to keep this risk in mind and strive actively to empower and gives voices to all the network members.

Networking narratives

5. Seeing inside

I said to her 'Why don't you do a regional networking conference in the women's prison?' Because nobody gets to see, I mean it's an open prison, it's not like a real prison; but actually, I did it because I thought, we're all doing this networking thing to make the city better, which I'm interested in anyway as a resident; but with all this power and influence, there's something about you that could be helpful for the prison. So, we did an event there and made a number of connections that I think still endure.

I asked a woman, Jackie, she was a lifer, if she would talk to these people and of course she was terrified. She was somebody who had been through the whole prison system and was up for a parole hearing. She was in an open prison, so she was on the right track. I just said:

> I think it's really important that they hear from somebody who has lived this, and is here as a resident. Not me talking about it. I have an experience of prison, for sure, but I've never been in. I don't really understand what it's like. You can't, without living it.

You know, at a level and a fairly deep level, but you can't *speak* like someone who's been through it. I asked her to speak, and I didn't tell them who she was. And she stood up, and she started, and it quickly became clear...and they were absolutely amazed. She said, 'I'm so nervous', and I said 'You're doing brilliantly'. When she went, I said, 'Now you know there's no questions about her offending or anything: this is just her experience'. Then somebody said, 'Will we be seeing anybody else from the prison?' And I said, 'Well, when you came in somebody took your coat, somebody gave you a lanyard, somebody made you a cup of tea, somebody showed you through. You haven't seen a member of staff'. And they could not believe that all of these women that they had interacted with, who were so professional, were prisoners.

Part of the reason I wanted to bring them in was just to demystify that, you know, there were these drugged-up violent women. They didn't see a member

> of staff all night. It was a massive source of 'Wow this has really opened our eyes', and, 'What can we do?' and all of that. And that was... that was an opportunity that I would never have had as the regional manager of the prison service, to convene that group of people. But once I was in that group of people, I could get them in the prison.
>
> There were a number of contracts within the prison; there was potential and I don't know where that went... certainly in terms of job opportunities. There were definitely a couple of those contacts made. There was probably a higher chance that they would be listened to and considered than before, where it would have just been: 'No. Ex-prisoner: no'. Because their picture of what that meant had changed.

Ask yourself?

1. What aspects of the criminal justice system do you feel can be described as 'wicked problems' and what kinds of local organisations could usefully be involved in solving these?
2. How might encounters of the kind described here change your own ideas of what community means?
3. What opportunities and concerns do you consider arise from these kinds of encounters, and from an ethical perspective, what are the risks and benefits?
4. What advice would you give to the speaker in terms of building and maintaining links between the prison and the network?

References

Bas, E. and Guillo, M. (2015) 'Particpatory Foresight for Social Innovation. Flux-3D Method,' *Technological Forecasting and Social Change* 101: 275–290, http://dx.doi.org/10.1016/j.techfore.2015.06.016

Bhatti, Z.A., Arain, G.A., Akram, M.S., Fang, Y. and Yasin, H.M. (2020) 'Constructive Voice Behavior for Social Change on Social Networking Sites: A Reflection of Moral Identity,' *Technological Forecasting and Social Change* 157: 120101, https://doi.org/10.1016/j.techfore.2020.120101

Budge, G., Mitchell, A., Rampling, T., Down, P. and The Bridge Collective. (2019) '"It Kind of Fosters a Culture of Interdependence": A Participatory Appraisal Study Exploring Participants' Experiences of the Democratic Processes of a Peer-Led Organisation,' *Journal of Community and Applied Social Psychology* 29: 178–192, https://doi.org/10.1002/casp.2393

Cockburn-Wootten, C., McIntosh, A.J., Smith, K. and Jefferies, S. (2018) 'Communicating across Tourism Silos for Inclusive Sustainable Partnerships,' *Journal of Sustainable Tourism* 26(9): 1483–1498, https://doi.org/10.1080/09669582.2018.1476519

Cajaiba-Santana, G. (2014) 'Social Innovation: Moving the Field Forward. A Conceptual Framework,' *Technological Forecasting and Social Change* 82: 42–51, http://dx.doi.org/10.1016/j.techfore.2013.05.008

Caron, C., Raby, R., Mitchell, C., Thewissen-Le Blanc, S. and Prioletta, J. (2017) 'From Concept to Data: Sleuthing Social Change-Orientated Youth Voices on You Tube,' *Journal of Youth Studies* 20(1): 47–62, https://doi.org/10.1080/13676261.2016.1184242

Davies, L. (2016) 'Wicked Problems: How Complexity Science Helps Direct Education Responses to Preventing Violent Extremism,' *Journal of Strategic Security* 9(4): 32–52, http://dx.doi.org/10.5038/1944-0472.9.4.1551

De La Pena, A. and Quintanilla, C. (2015) 'Share, Like and Achieve: The Power of Facebook to Reach Health Related Goals,' *International Journal of Consumer Studies* 39: 495–505, doi: 10.1111/ijcs.12224

Flick, C., Zamani, E.D., Stahl, B.C. and Brem, A. (2020) 'The Future of ICT for Health and Ageing: Unveiling Ethical and Social Issues through Horizon Scanning Foresight,' *Technological Forecasting and Social Change* 155: 119995, https://doi.org/10.1016/j.techfore.2020.119995

Frazer, R. and Watt, G. (2016) 'Pain, Politics and Volunteering in Tourism Studies,' *Annals of Tourism Research* 57: 176–189, http://dx.doi.org/10.1016/j.annals.2016.01.001

HERI (1996) *A Social Change Model of Leadership Development: Guidebook, version III.* Higher Education Research Institute, University of California Los Angeles.

Kleinhans, R. (2017) 'False Promises of Co-production in Neighbourhood Regeneration: The Case of Dutch Community Enterprises,' *Public Management Review* 19(10): 1500–1518, https://doi.org/10.1080/14719037.2017.1287941

Kuhns, L.M. and Ramirez-Valles, J. (2016) 'Creating Identity and Community: Latino Gay and Bisexual Men's Motives for Participation in the AIDS Movement,' *Journal of Community and Applied Social Psychology* 26: 32–46, doi: 10.1002/casp.2233

Linstone, H.A. (1969) 'When Is a Need a Need? The Problem of Normative Forecasting in a Changing Environment,' *Technological Forecasting* 1(1). This article was reprinted *Technological Forecasting and Social Change* 102 (2016): 2–10, http://dx.doi.org/10.1016/j.techfore.2015.11.014

Maxey, L., Henfrey, T., Chamberline, S., Bird, C. and Gonsalez, J. (2015) 'Radical Civic Transitions: Networking and Building Civic Solutions,' *ACME: An International E-Journal for Critical Geographies* 14(2): 431–441.

Minas, M., Ribeiro, M.T. and Anglin, J.P. (2019) 'Building Reciprocity: From Safety-Net to Social Transformation Programmes,' *Journal of Community and Applied Social Psychology* 1–21, doi: 10.1002/casp.2435

Munzel, A., Meyer-Waarden, L. and Galan, J.-P. (2018) 'The Social Side of Sustainability: Well-being as a Driver and an Outcome of Social Relationships and Interactions on Social Networking Sites,' *Technological Forecasting and Social Change* 130: 14–27, http://dx.doi.org/10.1016/j.techfore.2017.06.031

Rittel, H.W.J. and Webber, M.M. (1973) 'Dilemmas in a General Theory of Planning,' *Policy Science* 4: 155–169.

Sinapuelas, I.C. and Foo, N. H. (2019) 'Information Exchange in Social Networks for Healthcare,' *Journal of Consumer Marketing* 36(5): 692–702, http://dx.doi.org/10.1108/JCM-12-2017-2470

Stauss, K., Jackson, B.A. and Maxwell, D. (2019) 'Developing Networks in Disempowered Communities: Experiencing Hardships While Focusing on Opportunities,' *Journal of Community and Applied Social Psychology* 29: 402–417, https://doi.org/10.1002/casp.2408

Watson, L. and Fox, R. (2018) 'Adopting a Participatory Methodology and Post-structural Epistemology: Reflections on a Research Project with Young People,'

118 Networking for social change

Journal of Community and Applied Social Psychology 28: 471–482, https://doi.org/10.1002/casp.2380

Zoller, H.M. (2000) '"A Place You Haven't Visited Before": Creating the Conditions for Community Dialogue,' *Southern Journal of Communications* 65(2–3): 191–207.

Zoller, H.M. (2017) 'Health Activism Targeting Corporations: A Critical Health Communication Perspective,' *Health Communication* 32(2): 219–229, https://doi.org/10.1080/10410236.2015.1118735

6

NETWORKING AND PERSONAL GROWTH

Introduction: the strength of weak ties

Imagine a scenario where Amrit, a woman working in advertising and aged 29, has two close friends, Bonnie and Claire. Amrit has known Bonnie since the age of 11 when they started secondary school and they have grown up together. Claire became friendly with Amrit towards the end of their time in university, and they have a close bond based on a lot of shared interests. Being single, Amrit spends a lot of time with her friends and they all share a growing friendship circle. Although Bonnie and Claire are very different, they have been drawn together through their mutual relationship with Amrit; and, over time, they have come to find they have a lot of common interests. However, they both know that, in a sense, they have to get on well as they both enjoy spending time with Amrit.

In essence, this kind of scenario, illustrated in Figure 6.1, is the basis for a very important theory that was first set out in 1973 by Mark Granovetter, *The Strength of Weak Ties*. His theory is of particular relevance for this chapter as it has led to insights about how people pick up new ideas, learn new things and find new jobs. It is therefore worth looking at the theory in more detail as well as the work of later researchers who have built on, challenged and developed his thinking.

Granovetter (1973) describes 'strong ties' as characterised by:

- A significant amount of contact time between the people involved
- An intensity in emotions intensity
- Intimacy (in other words, how easily the people involved can share personal or sensitive information)
- Reciprocity

DOI: 10.4324/9781003026549-7

Viewpoint 6.1 Strength in weak ties

Well, I just like people. It's quite simple. I'm drawn to be friendly and approachable and I really strive to minimise the hierarchy and the power gradient with the people that I work with. As a result, I think if you treat people as people rather than as job roles, everyone's lives are enriched. Two minutes chit chat or a smile in the corridor at one end of the spectrum; and at the other end of the spectrum, how can something that we do together allow that person to blossom and go further and develop personally and professionally? Watching people take opportunities that you have exposed them to, you get a sense of, it sounds quite weird, of satisfaction or joy in the way that you're able to help somebody else.

FIGURE 6.1 Imagined personal network 1.

In the first part of his essay, Granovetter (1973) looks in detail at the relationship between the characters we are calling Bonnie and Claire. He suggests that for both to be good friends with Amrit, they must have considerable similarity. This increases the likelihood of friendship and the forming of a strong tie between Bonnie and Claire. It is possible that they might find they have little in common other than their friendship with Amrit, and thus they might only form a weak tie. He argues however that it is very unlikely they will form no tie at all. At this point, Granovetter includes a third relationship – a bridge. A bridge is a line in a network which provides the only path between two points – here, for example, from Amrit to Bonnie's sister's friend, Jan.

Bridges occur where there are weak ties; in this case, Amrit does not have a direct relationship with Jan but can reach her through her strong tie with Bonnie and weak tie with Bonnie's sister, Faye. Faye, the weak tie of Amrit's, is the bridge to Jan. Equally though, Bonnie (who obviously has a strong tie to her sister, Faye) has a weak tie to Faye's friend Jan. Imagine the situation where Amrit has a new product launch planned which might be of interest to the company for whom Faye works. Faye is based in finance so isn't able to help

Networking and personal growth

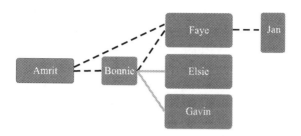

FIGURE 6.2 Imagined personal network 2.

directly, but Bonnie knows her sister's friend called Jan, who is a purchasing manager and would be a good person for Amrit to meet. So, if Amrit wants to reach Jan, she can either go through Faye or through Bonnie to Faye and thus to Jan (Figure 6.2).

So, as distance in the network increases, weak ties and bridges become more important in linking people to each other. The more weak ties there are in a network, the more local bridges there are also to create shorter pathways for people to connect with one another. The reason Granovetter set this out in so much detail is because he felt that studies to date had almost always focused on strong ties, focusing on relationships which respondents described as 'central'. Granovetter, who was interested in the ways that ideas are shared and spread, the diffusion of ideas, felt this was a mistake.

Weak ties and innovation

At the point at which Granovetter was writing, the early 1970s, it had been established in the literature that early innovators are often marginal characters, non-conformists. This is because well-established people at the centre of their networks are perceived to have more to lose by picking up a risky idea. One of Granovetter's great insights therefore is how marginal characters can easily spread innovative ideas, if they are on the edges of networks. This is the importance of the ideas of weak ties and bridges. Even though the innovators may have few strong ties, being marginal characters, they will nonetheless have a number of other ties which can be demonstrated to be effective in spreading new ideas. Granovetter gives a whole range of examples of this in practice; but perhaps the most interesting is that proposed by Milgram.

Stanley Milgram (1933–1984) is probably best known for his work at Yale University during the 1960s, where he carried out a series of experiments into obedience which are now deemed controversial in respect of their ethics. His relevance in this chapter is another well-known principle, although he didn't actually use this term – the so-called 'six degrees of separation'. In a series of publications from 1967, he appeared to demonstrate that all people are six or fewer connections away from one another. This work has been tested on a number of occasions since and usually

122 Networking and personal growth

holds up. For example, Bakhshandeh et al. (2011) found that, on average, the degree of separation between two random users on Twitter is 3.43, following an average 67 requests for information. Granovetter (1973) found Milgram's (1967) work to support his own, and in particular, used the definition Milgram drew between *friends* and *acquaintances* to correspond to his own use of strong and weak ties. Milgram found that reaching out to acquaintances rather than friends was more likely to end with the chain being completed – and the recipient target receiving the communication from the original sender.

Viewpoint 6.2 Putting people in touch

I am often asked to mentor people, and I often worry a bit about what their expectations are and why on earth they'd want me to mentor them. So, conversations I have with people are often very practical about 'what are the issues and the challenges you're facing? How can we how can we move this forward?' Often, I'll connect people together. So that's probably part of networking and in that situation, I don't think I owe anyone anything or anyone else feels I'm owing them anything. If I introduce two people and I know one is particularly keen to get involved in something, I might have a word with the other person first and say 'look I don't really know this person, so please vet them'. Or I might say to them: 'I do know this person; I think they might be of interest to you so feel free to consider them'. But what I'm not trying to do is use my connection there to say to somebody 'I've sorted you out a job so you owe me one' or anything like that. I'm absolutely clear I'm not doing it for those reasons; it's about connecting people together and helping to facilitate things.

Granovetter (1973) discusses a number of reasons why understanding the links between strong and weak ties matters. I will deal further below with its relevance specifically to career development, as that is of central interest to this chapter. Here, I want to draw attention to a further two important reasons. As we have seen above, he suggests that innovation, new ideas and even controversial arguments are more likely to be transmitted through weak ties, as such marginal members of the network are less likely to worry about reputational risk.

Granovetter also points out that groups that consist almost entirely of strong ties may be more inherently hostile to ideas coming from outside. He describes such groups as cliques that may in extreme conditions become quite isolated from new thinking or the diffusion of innovation. It follows from this that any individual who is interested in personal growth may want to include weak ties within their own networks, to expose themselves to thinking which may challenge their own ideas and be generative of new insights.

Viewpoint 6.3 Picking up new ideas

I'm quite an opinionated person, so I need alternative views to help me enrich my understanding. I tend to make decisions and stick to them, because if you're not driving forward, you're just flying around. But sometimes it might not be right and having people that can say 'Had you thought of this?' does allow you to choose a better path or refashion what you're doing.

It's serendipity really. I've always found that when I did go for things with a specific agenda, I found it very uncomfortable, I didn't enjoy it. But if you go with an open mind – as I say, with these things the networking is around the peripheries of something else. It's the 15 minutes before whatever you've gone there for, and the 30 minutes afterwards, that I've found most enjoyable and most productive.

Second, Granovetter (1973) argues that the nature of the social networks that make up communities can have a big impact on whether or not a particular community is able to mobilise for the common good. His discussion concludes that factors such as geographic immobility and lifelong friendships may make it more difficult for the small networks embedded in these communities to use weak ties and bridges. For Granovetter, the internal makeup of the various social networks in a larger community is of lesser importance to the ability of each network to make linkages with others.

Using ties for career advancement

The Strength of Weak Ties (Granovetter, 1973) is mainly known in relation to the use of weak ties for finding a new job. Granovetter wanted to explore the commonly held view that American blue-collar workers are more likely to find out about new jobs through personal contacts; having previously established this was true for higher-level professionals (Granovetter, 1970). What his 1973 study adds is a clear understanding of how these mechanisms actually work. Markedly, his empirical research demonstrated that crucial job-related information overwhelmingly came through weak ties: old colleagues, friends of friends and people outside the work-based networks. He concluded that weak ties are thus central to worker mobility and to linking work-based networks more coherently.

Granovetter followed up his early work with a more substantial publication in 1974, *Getting a Job: A Study of Contacts and Careers*, republished in 1995. His research found that information leading to job changes flowed through informal channels, often leading to better outcomes than more formal recruitment methods. Unsurprisingly, people with rich work-centred networks tended to do better than people who relied in the main on family and friends. What is

124 Networking and personal growth

added in this later work is more attention to the roles of power and influence in this process: better outcomes occur for those with a strong advantage in the job market and access to more powerful contacts. This has clear ethical implications, which maybe resonate more strongly for the contemporary reader, about those who historically tend to lack access to these kinds of networks. But Granovetter was not advocating for the use of these methods of job seeking; rather, he was recording what he found at the time in the 1970s in the US. In his later work, he critiqued the failure of economic theory to understand the extent to which economic actions related to social issues rather than operating in the kinds of idealised markets imagined by economics academics. His afterword to the second edition (Granovetter, 1995) recommends further work to understand the ways that network processes produce and sustain social inequality.

Viewpoint 6.4 Finding a job by networking

The funniest for example which actually might be relevant, is my current role as chief operating officer at a company which is based in London, which came about totally by accident. Because one of the co-founders of that business was sitting on a panel for an economic breakfast briefing that I organised every quarter, and I thought what he said was incredibly interesting and insightful and wrote him a fairly naff email afterwards saying how interested I'd been by everything that he said. And what I wanted to do was to organise for him to come in and run some round tables for our retail occupier clients, and what he actually did was phone me up and say 'We're looking for a chief operating officer. Would you be interested?'

Well, it wasn't terribly formal. I met with him over a beer and had a chat, and then I met with his co-founder over a coffee and had a chat, and then they offered me the job. Having obviously reviewed my CV and taken four references as well, so that was the formal bit of it if you like.

Granovetter's (1973) work on the use of social networks in job seeking was developed and extended by Brown and Konrad (2001). Their contribution was to contrast how individuals looked for jobs in a sector where jobs were growing in comparison to a sector where jobs were in decline. In declining industries, job seekers are more likely to use strong ties for their job hunt. This, they argue, is because job seekers need to open up more about the difficulties they are encountering in sectors where job opportunities are fewer. However, over time, the job hunter turned to weaker ties, possibly sourcing those connections through people with whom they have stronger ties. Their research supports the need for enhanced networking for those in declining industries who need a new job. Unsurprisingly, in flourishing sectors where jobs are growing, the researchers found there were far more networking opportunities available; and thus it was easier to make contact

Networking and personal growth **125**

through weak ties. Where jobs are scarce, therefore, the research concluded that job seekers had to work harder to use their networks, deploying both strong and weak ties. From a practical perspective, Brown and Konrad (2001) emphasise the importance of stepping out of the comfort zone when jobs are hard to find and connecting with people well beyond the usual circle of friends and close acquaintances.

More recently, the digital platform, LinkedIn, uses different levels of connections to put people in touch with one another. Their platform demonstrates how strong ties can lead to weak ties and bridges. Davis et al. (2020) examined how people use LinkedIn for career self-management. Among the things they explored were networking ability (competence) as well as networking usage (frequency). The outcomes they were interested in covered a range of career growth issues: help with work, career sponsorship, social support, job search, business assistance, political guidance and information and ideas. They found that all these outcomes were observable for people who used LinkedIn frequently. In contrast, the number of contacts was found not to be important in terms of the benefits realised. What drives benefits realisation from LinkedIn is frequent usage, and this includes the passive absorption of new ideas, information and contacts through reading the posts of others. More important than what an individual puts on their own profile is the ability to know who to contact for relevant information, together with understanding how best to make contact with them.

Viewpoint 6.5 Three perspectives on connecting online

Person A: I am very selective about who I connect with so I will only connect with people that I know. So, I don't use it as a business winning, or a platform in, in that sense. I do use it to contact people that I've lost contact with and don't have an email address for, pretty frequently.

Person B: Yeah, I quite like LinkedIn. I think it needs to be used sparingly. That's probably not the right word but with circumspection and logically, sensibly rather than the blunderbuss approach that some people seem to have with it.

Person C: The problem with LinkedIn is that it's people putting a face to the world, it's not very intimate and people write stuff about the exciting things they're doing or their interesting points of view on issue this and issue, that so it's quite useful for, you know, what the professional conversation is about: but it doesn't really give you very good insights because everybody's trying to put their best face on.

Using networks for personal development

Our survey research supports the findings of Davis et al. (2020). Motivations for networking were varied, as might be predicted. The most popular (indicated by 85% of respondents on a tick list) was learning from others, with an emphasis on

126 Networking and personal growth

new ideas (78%) and different perspectives (70%). Emotional motives also featured, with over half of respondents indicating peer support and more than one in four using networking to 'let off steam'.

In a similar way to the research literature we have discussed in this chapter, our research also found that respondents used personal networking to help them gain recognition in the circles in which they wanted to become known. We call this IN-crowding, and for convenience, we reproduce our definition below:

In-crowding: We use this term to cover all the outcomes suggested by respondents in terms of wanting to belong to an 'in-crowd' or a group considered to be opinion leaders or influencers within a given field or sector. The outcome sought by the individual concerned is to gain credibility or advantage through association with people seen as leaders or holding some kind of power valued by others.

Viewpoint 6.6 Joining the in-crowd

I definitely got better at it in the centre of the civil service because it's an activity that a lot of people do. Whereas in the field it would be seen as, well, 'what's the purpose? It's not going to get the task done'. Whereas in the centre it was… somebody once said to me this thing that I've never forgotten, and I didn't agree with, but I thought, 'ah right, I get it'. He said that somebody had said to him, and this is why he networked so much: 'If you're not spending at least half of your week having coffee with people you are not doing the job'. And I thought that epitomised the difference between that policy Whitehall environment and the operational more distant 'If you're not doing your job, you're wasting your time'. Your job was task, whereas theirs was, or part of the job was, networking. That's very long and convoluted, but I just found it incredibly stark – the difference within the same organisation.

Additionally, as we have discussed above, we found that inside the wider professional networks deployed by individuals for their own personal learning and career development, people may also have an 'inner circle' network of more trusted contacts, with relatively strong ties based on friendships and affinity. While our respondents told us that this group may offer credibility and advantage in career terms on occasion, they offered a lot more as well: sharing learning, opening up about problems and providing mutual support, often over a period of many years. Whereas IN- crowding is based on recognising the perceived power and status of key individuals in the network to others in a similar sector, IN-sight is based on a personal recognition of the value of the contact to the individual actor.

Insight: The outcome sought is to reinforce the ideas or ideals that an individual already holds for mutual support, or by mixing with like-minded others in order to strengthen and confirm their current world view. Through networking

Networking and personal growth **127**

activity, the individual is helped to deepen, shape and better align beliefs, attitudes and behaviours. This is sometimes a defensive strategy for peers who share common pressures and who can thus support and maintain a collective sanity in an otherwise chaotic universe.

These two related but different motivations for developing strong personal networks will be explored in more detail in the rest of this chapter.

We have observed in previous chapters that it is easier for research studies to examine the structures, missions and processes of networks at an organisational level than to examine what it is the individuals actually do within the network and to evaluate the benefits that arise from these activities. The sheer volume of potential actors, the variety of network forms, the transitory and informal nature of individual practice, all these are constraints on the research process. A limitation to many studies, acknowledged by the researchers, is the extent to which their findings may or may not be generalisable to populations outside the ones they have researched. With that caveat, what can we learn from the literature about effective networking at an individual level?

Kim (2013) looked at how people network, when they are doing so with the intention of advancing their career. Her work sets out to determine what enables and what constrains effective networking practice. Furthermore, she considers how networking may develop over time in a dynamic way. Summarising her work, she breaks it down into two phases: building and maintaining.

In Phase One, individual networkers engage in two activities: socialising and getting involved. Socialising can happen in a number of ways, both inside and outside an organisation, for example, quite casually in informal chat or through deliberately attending events that promote getting to know one another. Getting involved would include joining something called a network or a professional association, or taking part in a project or perhaps committing to a regular and structured set of activities.

In Phase Two, Kim (2013) distinguishes between self-prioritisation behaviour and Other-prioritisation. Most networkers seemed to display both these behaviours at different times. Self-prioritisation behaviours include talking about past achievements and current responsibilities, sharing career hopes and ambitions and being willing to get involved in new things. Other-prioritisation behaviours are things like working out what someone else needs and helping them to get it (say through sharing information) or helping others by delivering on outcomes or goals. Relationships are maintained through a variety of keeping in touch mechanisms at regular or irregular intervals. Kim's work (2013) stresses the longitudinal nature of this kind of networking activity.

Kim (2013) identifies four outcomes from networking for the individual actors: access to greater unwritten information, greater visibility, legitimacy (credibility with a wider group of influential people) and reputation. She does however point out that these outcomes are not guaranteed. There are all sorts of reasons why the other party may not pursue the initial contact or may not sustain it for long. The practical implication of this is the need to keep developing new

128 Networking and personal growth

contacts in parallel with trying to deepen and sustain older relationships. Strategic decisions may sometimes need to be taken about the choices to be made at a particular point – to go broader or to go deeper. Kim's central message is that networking needs to be seen as a dynamic process and as one to be managed – it's not enough to just be highly proactive about the contacts to be made. She emphasises the *exchange* notion in networking, which we discuss elsewhere as reciprocity. Networking requires cooperation from others to be successful; so it therefore follows that the networker should attend to the needs and outcomes of others as well as themselves (Box 6.1).

BOX 6.1 THE BUSINESS IMPACT OF USING PERSONAL TIES

Romero (2018) explores the relationship between personal and business relations in the biotechnology sector in four regions of Chile. The purpose of the research was to identify how intra-cluster business relations emerge and to assess if the personal network structure in which the cluster is embedded determines the intra-cluster business network structure. In other words, is there a positive relationship between personal and business links?

Compared to other countries in Latin America, Chile has high levels of income per capita and its institutions are highly grounded on the rule of law. Despite the relative stability of the economic indicators in the country, the evidence suggests that personal relations provide additional information about firms in the market that is useful for the generation of business relations between organisations. These results have a negative side. Given that personal relations within the cluster are important for the creation of business linkages between firms, it might be that clusters show a lock-in of knowledge in the long term, which may lead to the creation of business cliques. If this is the case, firms not only face difficulties in terms of R&D uncertainties and financial restrictions, but also must access the 'right' social network if they are to grow. These findings support the notion that there are drawbacks in terms of personal relations for cluster growth.

Personality types

When it comes to thinking about networking, some respondents in our research told us that they weren't good at networking as they didn't have 'that kind of personality'. It is often suggested that extraverts are the natural networkers, but is this the case? Are there aspects of people's personalities that enable them to network more effectively?

These questions were researched by Wolff and Kim (2012). They used the Big Five framework of personality dimensions (Goldberg, 1990). This framework suggests the following five dimensions:

- Extraversion
- Agreeableness
- Openness to experience
- Conscientiousness
- Emotional stability

Viewpoint 6.7 I'm just not the type

Actually, I don't actively network. I'm a bit of an introvert, so I don't really go out looking. Well, what do I mean by that? Yeah, I like some people but there are not many (laughs) so I don't go out looking for loads.

Their findings suggest that extraversion and openness to experience relate most closely to networking behaviours, reinforcing the social and informational importance of networks to individuals (Wolff and Kim, 2012). This emphasis on the *exchange* notion of networks is an important part of what they find to be significant from their research. While extroverts are good at building contacts, they tend to pay less attention to maintaining relationships. Interestingly, agreeableness correlates more closely with internal networking (across organisational silos) than to networking beyond the organisation. Openness to experience, it is suggested, is effective in terms not just of building contacts, but also in maintaining and developing them. Conscientiousness doesn't correlate closely with networking activity, perhaps because such individuals are more likely to concentrate on the specific tasks they are charged with doing. Finally, the affective dimension specifically is not highly relevant to effective networking, and the authors (Wolff and Kim, 2012) surmise this may be because such individuals privilege fewer, stronger ties over a network of weaker ties.

Caution must be exercised in practical terms, when any reader of this present book thinks about their own networking behaviour. It is not the case that only individuals who display extraversion and openness to new ideas can become effective networkers. Rather, research like this helps someone who wants to develop their networking ability to recognise the aspects of their personality that might help or hinder this and pay attention to these features in planning their strategy. So, for example, a highly extrovert person may want to stop and think how they can ensure that they hold onto valuable contacts in the longer term. They might want to check their enthusiasm for building lots of new relationships in favour of spending relatively more time extending and developing the contacts they already have.

Furthermore, personality type is only one aspect of networking. Context is a second one, with the environment and life stage also impacting on the ability to

130 Networking and personal growth

network at a given time. Finally, for want of a better word, we need to consider 'fit': how well a particular network fits an individual's needs, given the balance of all these factors.

Viewpoint 6.8 Friends for life

Now we were colleagues in the same office, so our relationship started by finding ourselves like-minded about the political atmosphere we were in; and we used to have lunch and it was very helpful indeed to be able to exchange views and have a laugh which we couldn't do in the office. And since then we... we both went our separate ways in career terms, but we still met you know and a frequent topic of discussion was what we called 'the Theatre of the Workplace', and it was really a kind of satirical look at the way people behaved: and it was extremely entertaining and helpful to know that there were other people who thought the same as you, you didn't have to take other people's behaviour seriously: and in many ways, finding an ally like that is essential to keep your sense of identity or you get lost.

Network 'fit' and the individual

In Chapter 1 we considered, among other variables, choices of network depending on like/unlike pairings. More formally, this is called homophily/heterophily in the research literature, and is concerned with the extent to which individuals (either through chance or by choice) prefer to be with people who are more like them or the converse. Research has shown that networks can perpetuate inequalities (Ibarra et al., 2005, 2010, McGuire, 2012); but equally, individuals may network with people like themselves to collectively support one another in combatting perceived disadvantages (examples of these are given in Boxes 6.2 and 6.3).

BOX 6.2 WIDENING ACCESS TO ONLINE NETWORKING

The *Universal Access in the Information Society* journal addresses the accessibility, usability and, ultimately, acceptability of Information Society Technologies by anyone, anywhere, at any time and through any media and device. Its relevance to this present chapter is the insight it offers into how digital communities can potentially form where people can find people like themselves. Equally too though, it discusses barriers and challenges from the perspective of the end user.

One such study was conducted in Slovenia with deaf and hard of hearing people. The authors point out that such individuals have communication specificities compared with hearing users such as using not only written and spoken language, but also sign language. Hitherto, there has been a lack of research and understanding of the end users' needs of this group from the people who design technology for social networking. One gap in understanding is the difference in the group between the deaf, including those born deaf, and the hard of hearing. This may include not just a preference for sign language or not, but also varying levels of discomfort about their competence in both written and spoken language.

Sometimes, deaf people will refer to themselves as deaf (in lower case), which relates to their audiological status, from being hard of hearing to being profoundly deaf. Some members will also self-identify as Deaf (in upper case), which is a reference to being a member of a community who share both language and culture. Failing to understand this complexity will limit the usability of the platform for some users, thus restricting their ability to network with others like themselves. However, the research reports that the use of social media is significantly associated with the desire to network and build community online with people like themselves, for this group. This contributes to self-esteem and the reduction of stigma.

Sources: Universal Access in the Information
Society Kožuh et al. (2015).

It could be argued that 20 years into the new millennium, HR processes now combat the negative aspects of homophily and are inherently fairer. Globally, there is still little evidence that things have changed significantly, with white men continuing to dominate the upper echelons of most organisations; so it is worth spending a bit of time thinking why this may be the case. It is argued that, for example, women spend less time networking because they experience greater time pressures as a result of family responsibilities (Forret and Dougherty, 2001) and that they tend to use networking more for social support, whereas men network more to promote their self-interests (Forret and Dougherty, 2004). While at a general level these trends may be observable, it is important to look at why and how networks and networking activity may reinforce these trends and perpetuate inequality even where they look to combat it.

Van Den Brink and Benschop (2014) looked at this issue in relation to higher-level career development in women academics in Dutch universities. Their work is interesting because of its approach to gender. Rather than seeing male and female as two opposing characteristics, they argue that gender in networks needs to be viewed as a social practice, not a binary variable. Their emphasis on social practices is concerned with what people say or do in relation to network activities. The particular practice that is the focus of their discussion is 'gatekeeping', which is the way people in key positions operate when they are scouting for suitable candidates for professorial roles through formal and informal networks. They argue that gatekeeping is a gendering practice, usually carried out by men,

132 Networking and personal growth

and favouring homophily, that is, people like themselves. In these gendered practices, the gatekeepers distinguish between men and women in routine, often unconscious ways. Most tellingly, they demonstrate that the senior women (the exception in these circles) may emulate men, choosing to exhibit the same gatekeeper behaviours so as not to stand out or be perceived differently in their peer group (Van Den Brink and Benschop, 2014).

It might be argued that 'gatekeeping' is inherently the same as 'in-crowding', but we see a difference. In the case of 'in-crowding', it is the networker who selects who it is that they wish to get to know, and in the case of 'gatekeeping', the opposite is true – it is the ones who have power who decide who will be admitted to their circle. It is interesting to look more closely at the behaviours that Van Den Brink and Benschop (2014) specifically identify with gatekeeping:

- Inviting and nominating
- Asking for recommendations from their existing networks
- Building reputations (the academics with higher status are the most likely to be invited to be gatekeepers)
- Identifying with the similar
- Reproducing the proven success model
- Creating opportunities expressly for women

This last point needs further development. At first glance, it might look as though the gatekeepers are aware of their gendered practices and are actively working to change them, and up to a point, this is true. But what Van Den Brink and Benschop (2014) found in their work is that it is not necessarily the case. In response to the lack of women in professorial positions in Dutch universities, several of these universities have expressly set up Chairs for women candidates. However, these Chairs are personal Chairs, tend to be temporary positions and have less status and power than full Chairs.

Forret and Dougherty (2004) investigated specifically what types of networking behaviours were beneficial in terms of career development and then examined whether or not they advantaged men, women or both. Depressingly, they found certain behaviours were effective for men, but none that were effective for women. The positive behaviours they identified were socialising, engaging in professional activities and increasing internal visibility. In their discussion, they suggest that the reasons for this might be that women don't network with sufficiently powerful people, perhaps that men are more effective at demanding recognition for taking on further professional activities or women may be more hesitant in asking their contacts for career assistance.

These preceding paragraphs should not be seen as an argument against networking for women or for any other group who are disadvantaged in career advancement in their sector. Rather, it is a call to action in terms of being more strategic about your networking practice. If the issue for you is that you are not using your network to full advantage, then that is something to address. Such strategies might include working on increasing self-confidence and building social capital (De Clerk and Verreynne, 2017). If alternatively, you are perhaps in the wrong network, then study how your competitor candidates are using networking to gain advantage. Finally, it is important to focus on what benefits you want from networking and how to realise them. Networking is not only about promotion or increased pay, it is just as much about support, friendship and personal learning.

BOX 6.3 DO WOMEN NETWORK DIFFERENTLY TO MEN: WHAT DOES THE RESEARCH TELL US?

Networking for female business leaders

This large Scandinavian study set out to explore the kinds of contacts and networks women find supportive in their role as business leaders and which also support their willingness to grow their business. The results showed that personal networks are seen as a more supportive asset than business networks; that personal contacts with other entrepreneurs are regarded as valuable; and that women entrepreneurs who are positive towards new networks already have a more heterogenic network than those who do not express this willingness (Bogren et al., 2013).

Business women in Cyprus

This study from Cyprus aimed to investigate the importance of networking with regard to women's progression in the workplace as well as the barriers women are faced with in their attempt to play the networking game according to male rules. It is clear that women are restricted from networking opportunities either intentionally or due to cultural and societal norms, and this resulted in minimising their chances of breaking the glass ceiling and progressing to the top of the organisational ladder (Socratous, 2018).

Muslim women in the UK

This research explored the personal networks of second-generation, British-born, Muslim female entrepreneurs. It found that the personal networks of second-generation female entrepreneurs of Pakistani origin are a product of gender, culture and religion, where choices in kinship, friendship and business or professional ties in those networks are underpinned by the complex mix of gender, culture and religion. This should contribute to a critical and a more nuanced understanding of female and minority entrepreneurship (Mitra and Basit, 2019).

134 Networking and personal growth

> *How gender affects networking behaviour*
>
> The purpose of this Dutch study was to gain insight into the relations between gender, networking behaviour and network structure in order to investigate the relevance of gender for organizational networks. The results showed that the men account managers employ exchange and affect-based trust networking and, to a lesser extent, authoritative networking, whereas the women account managers employ affect-based trust and also use exchange. The practical application of this is to support organization members to employ the diversity of networking behaviours necessary to generate optimal network structures and outcomes, thinking more about how network relationships are fostered and grown (Gremmen et al., 2013).

Motivation and networking

Networking can be a powerful force for individuals who may feel, in some sense, 'stuck' on their journey through life. There are many reasons why anyone can have a period of feeling demotivated, diminished or not in control of their lives. Recognising there is a problem is a good start to working on a solution, but taking the first steps to move on can be hard. Networks can be a powerful resource at these times. As we have already seen, they are relatively informal; bring together people from very disparate backgrounds who might not otherwise meet; and they operate on a principle of reciprocity. So, reaching out to your networks for advice and support in these more barren periods can be an effective strategy to revitalise your curiosity, energy and self-motivation.

One explanation of how this works is the self-determination theory (Ryan and Deci, 2000). If you are experiencing a sense of apathy or alienation in your personal growth and social development, it is well worth looking into this theory in more depth, as space precludes a fuller discussion of it here.

Self-determination theory (Ryan and Deci, 2000) looks at a spectrum of motivation, with intrinsic motivation (self-determined and generative of creativity and learning) as the highest form. Motivation, they argue, concerns energy, direction, persistence and the ability to be productive. Ryan and Deci discuss this broadly as an interaction between three factors: autonomy or personal control over their actions, allied with a sense of competence (efficacy in their actions). This sense of competence or lack of competence is either positively or negatively influenced by factors in the environment, demonstrating that social conditions are significant in the development of feelings of both autonomy and competence. Thus, they posit the third factor relevant to the development of motivation is relatedness; that sense of security and belonging that starts in the family and in schools and goes on into adult life, relationships

Networking and personal growth **135**

and the world of work. The ideal formula can be expressed as the ABC of intrinsic motivation:

- Autonomy
- Belonging
- Competence

As few of us will experience the ideal formula at every stage of our lives, Ryan and Deci (2000) discuss variations of their theme across a range of different possibilities. The relevance of self-determination theory to this present work is their belief that motivation can be increased even in poor conditions, where individuals attempt to internalise what is being asked of them (which they are reluctant to take on) by developing greater self-regulation over their actions. So, an individual can move from a state of rejecting the desired outcomes to accepting them to a greater or lesser extent, which can help to increase personal satisfaction.

How might we use the theory of self-determination to consider how networking could help an individual rediscover their motivation? There are a number of possibilities, depending on how alienated the individual may feel at any particular time.

1. At the most extreme, an individual may feel wholly demotivated, lacking in control and without worth. Here, networking can provide an alternative locus for action. This action could take the form of an active job search of the kind discussed above, to replace the poor conditions with something better. Equally though, it could take an individual into another arena of action, perhaps engaging in social change of the kind discussed in Chapter 5. Feeling competent and belonging in a different context may contribute to rebuilding motivation in the problem area.

2. Less extremely, someone may be suffering from a degree of burn out at work. Having come into a job with high hopes for an interesting and stimulating career, such an individual may feel organisationally constrained, having to comply with a plethora of rules and regulations and overly subject to management rewards and punishments. Here, the kinds of networking activities which might restore motivation could include peer-to-peer networking, exploring and sharing experiences with others to better understand what is happening. If this is a normal career phase, accepting it as such will help an individual to understand why they need to do whatever it is they need to do to get past it. This might be, for example, passing some necessary exams to lead to promotion. However, if the experience proves not typical in that peer group, the individual will be motivated to move on. Here, the peer group can be utilised in the formation of a career change plan, possibly actively brokering introductions or signalling opportunities.

136   Networking and personal growth

3. Equally, though, for this same situation, an older mentor in a work-based network can give a different kind of support. From their perspective, they will be able to demonstrate the opportunities that lie further along the road. Perhaps they may open up new professional directions that were previously not known (e.g. leaving the front line to go into a training role, changing offices, changing teams). There are always more possibilities that can present to the perspective of a single individual: networks can open up multiple perspectives. A mentor may be able to point to further resources that could help new learning, rebuilding a sense of autonomy and competence. Additionally, the validation from a respected 'elder' that such dry periods are a part of working life can be useful in helping someone work through them.

4. A third situation may arise at times of significant change – either personal or professional. It is natural to look back to the 'good old days' when things seemed stable or better understood. Change can seem threatening, difficult or unwanted. Reaching out to others in very different situations serves as a reminder that change is always with us. Despite the diversity of personal experience, the change journey can be strikingly similar. Motivation, at times of significant change, tends to be restored when an individual starts to see the worth of the new actions. Once the direction of change is valued and internalised, relevant to the personal growth of the self, then the motivation to learn new ways of working is renewed. Listening and talking to others can be helpful in terms of enabling a personal understanding of the change process, the impact of change on the self and the potential for new opportunities.

Viewpoint 6.9 A starting place

Something that I did naturally was find an informal mentor, early. They are usually quite keen to help as well. I mentor people on a free basis and keep an interest in how they are going. I think that works really well. I think that is part of networking: to find a mentor, an older person, somebody who has been there and done it, and can help and guide you. Because the only way to beat the system, and to be good at networking is to learn how to do it.

This brief application of self-determination theory to networking is designed to reinforce the point that individuals can use their networks very flexibly, to support their very personal goals in terms of growth and self-determination. Thinking more carefully about your needs can help you to find the right kind of activity for you at a given moment, recognising this will be a changing thing. Personal networks (as we see in the imaginary example of Amrit and friends) work best in informal and sociable settings. They thus can feel like a comfortable starting point from which to embark on personal change.

Practical implications

The biggest problem for many people is that having recognised the value of networking, they are not sure where to start. Luckily, there are lots of useful self-help books out there that are full of good ideas. In this next section, we will point you to those and share some of their suggestions to get you started.

The first of these is by the business guru Tom Peters, and this is not a book about networking at all. Tom Peters is probably best known for his work *Thriving on Chaos* (1988) which forecasts the incredible turbulence which would affect the world of work in the next two decades. His 1999 book, *Reinventing Work: the Brand You 50*, is written for individuals in such a new world of work, who will move flexibly from project to project, managing their own careers through networking. While, for many, the world of work has not yet transformed itself in this way, others are already thriving in their portfolio careers. Whatever your personal circumstances, this book offers lots of ideas for getting started. Written in bullet points, short bursts and lists, it's both fun and quite practical. More importantly, it's the sort of book that you can dip into and choose the bits which work for you.

We draw your attention particularly to Chapter 22, which is about nurturing your networks (containing the now quaint idea of the Rolodex which is an old-style contacts record!). Peters reminds us of the importance of reciprocity, a theme we have referred to again and again in this present work:

> So, are you care-ful (full of care)…towards your Network? Do you nurture them? (*Unfailingly?*) Come to their assistance? (*Unfailingly?*) Check on their wellbeing? (*Unfailingly?*).
>
> *(Peters, 1999, p. 109, his emphasis)*

If you are in doubt about how to get started in a network or how to make the first move towards someone you want to get to know better, an excellent way to begin is to see whether you can do something for them. It will always feel easier to offer something than to ask for something, and most people will respond warmly to such an approach. Elsewhere in the same book, Peters makes the point that you need to keep these suggestions current – a recent article, a new contact, a programme that will be coming up in the next few days. So, in keeping current in order to offer ideas through your networks, you are keeping yourself in touch with new ideas and new thinking too.

In a similar vein, Dexter and Wilson (2017) have a chapter on what they call Networlding Support Exchange. All that means is that you spend time and effort ensuring that all your network communications are a two-way process, starting with active listening. Their book also contains a chapter on planning your networking strategy, another idea we recommend above. Again, this chapter offers some practical tips to get going:

- Allow serendipities to happen (about taking advantage of lucky breaks and opportunities)

138 Networking and personal growth

- Look at your career in three-year increments (different planning horizons)
- Throw yourself a challenge (about stepping out of your comfort zone, also recommended by Peters (1999))
- Get visible
- Be helpful

They also add the useful reminder to be selective – not to think about quantity but quality. We endorse this, as one thing will usually lead to another. If your problem is that first step, then do work on a strategy but bear in mind the obvious point that all great strategies start with a first step.

The obvious first step is to attend a networking event. While you could attend any just to get started, it makes more sense to do some research and try to find one that is likely to be a good starting place. Stephan Thomas (2016) has some suggestions about how you might do this, if you don't know already. But, equally, you might not begin with a designated 'networking event'. An alternative might be to identify someone you admire and to whom you are already connected through strong or weak ties. Ask your tie to introduce you to the person you admire and ask that person what their recommendations might be to support you to network effectively. This is not a big favour to ask and they may even invite you to attend something with them and make some early introductions.

Mark Kreiger (in Redler (ed) 2020) then has some advice for what you do when you get to the right event, which we have summarised:

- Be well prepared – on time, correctly dressed
- Don't socialise – look for people who want to network
- Ask them what they do and listen to the answer
- Be warm and let them talk about themselves
- Think about a connection that might help them (we would add or an article etc.)
- Follow up the next day

Viewpoint 6.10 Talking to strangers

Be yourself, be authentic, be genuine, be a human being. Understand the fact that most people engage at a personal level rather than anything else and so that is always the starting point. Don't pre-rehearse, because that never comes across as being natural. Ask open questions because actually most people quite like talking about themselves and what they do, and that is a very easy way into a conversation; that then enables you to work out whether there is a conversation at a business level or whether it's just somebody who you quite enjoy having a conversation with.

Networking and personal growth **139**

To this, he adds the advice to go for fewer, more genuine, follow ups and to be sincere. Stefan Thomas (2016) adds that there is no point in networking if you don't follow up (p. 85). He suggests a variety of ways you could do this, including using technology to help you track and manage your networks.

Conclusion

This chapter considers networking in a very personal way: thinking about how an individual can both gain and confer benefits through networking across their personal and professional life. There are specific ways that networking can help people: directly in terms of finding a job or learning relevant things to gain promotion, and also indirectly by helping maintain self-identity, regain motivation or work as a mentor to others. For those readers who have now reached the end of the work, we would close by emphasising a message that we hope has been clear throughout: there is no one single way, a right way or a wrong way to network. Networking means different things and works in different ways in different places. There is however one common message: you have to begin it, to be in it.

Networking narratives

6. Aiming to change the world

I'm pissed off, as a black woman, that there are very few black women, and black men, in senior roles in organisations, and that as a younger person, I always thought if I worked harder blah blah, blah blah blah, then you would get opportunities. But it doesn't actually work like that.

Some of those things that are linked I suppose to Critical Race Theory, in the sense that rather than that liberal place of 'We're all equal. People will understand and treat us equitably', the reality is it ain't gonna happen. So, how do we manage that in ways that allow people to fulfil their potential rather than spending many, many years working very hard, spending a lot of money on extra qualifications, which means people spend a lot of time away from their family, and doing the things that they all should do, thinking that that will be recognised when it isn't?

Yes, I want a better life for my kids and my grandkids actually.

Very recently actually, I've been working with white men in their late 40s, early 50s. They're the ones who have the power and have to do things differently. Rather than just talking about issues, so it's been about... overly... over the summer because of the murder of George Floyd and then the Black Lives Matter events.

I advertised on LinkedIn and did a number of free seminar things looking at race issues and discussing race issues. The thing about racism initiatives in organisations is that they are often geared at people from black and minority ethnic communities, therefore the people in the less powerful place rather than the people with the power who have got to do things differently. No matter how much women do in that less powerful place, no matter how much people from black communities do in that less powerful place, unless you've got people in the more powerful place engaged, you ain't gonna change anything.

So they are, if you like, a couple of people who responded to those sessions who were genuinely saying 'So what do I need to do?'. I am still linked with them. It has helped me frame some of the things I do rather differently because they are the people I need to get to change. They're the ones who need to listen and do things differently if there are going to be real changes.

So, if I'm talking about creating an inclusive environment, talking to these people they want four points; 'What are the four things you need to do? Can you give me four things to do', just like that! Now it's much more complicated than that, as we know. But before, I couldn't have been bothered about making it manageable for that group of people to understand because they were a lost cause in my view. But I have met a few who are not yet a lost cause. So yeah, I am linked with these two anyway…I have written a couple of bits and pieces that I want people like these two guys to understand, and that's where they hang out.

I'm a bit old-fashioned, so I'm still on boring old things like emails. I know I should be using … MailChimp and all those. Actually I'm never gonna use MailChimp. I did look at that and there's no way I'm having a chimp at the bottom of my emails, but that's another thing.

Ask yourself?

1. How active are you in trying to understand things from the perspective of others and to engage with and use their language and way of seeing things?
2. How might you find supportive networks to help you manage specific barriers to your professional success?
3. What advice would you give the speaker on extending her work with white men?
4. What strategies should networks in particular employ to ensure that all members can feel equally welcome and equally able to participate authentically?
5. How can you use the ideas in this chapter to start or improve your networking skills?

References

Bakhshandeh, R., Samadi, M., Azimifar, Z. and Schaeffer, J. (2011) 'Degrees of Separation in Social Networks,' *Proceedings of the 4th Annual Symposium on Combinatorial Search, SoCS 2011* [Online]. Available at: https://www.researchgate.net/publication/220743668_Degrees_of_Separation_in_Social_Networks (Accessed 17 March 2021).

Bogren, M., Von Friedrichs, Y., Rennemio, O. and Widding, O. (2013) 'Networking Women Entrepreneurs: Fruitful for Business Growth?' *International Journal of Gender and Entrepreneurship* 5(1): 60–77, doi: 10.1108/17566261311305210

Brown, D.W. and Konrad, A.S. (2001) 'Granovetter Was Right,' *Group & Organization Management* 26(4): 434–462, doi: 10.1177/1059601101264003

Davis, J., Wolff, H-G., Forret, M. and Sullivan, S. (2020) 'Networking via LinkedIn: An Examination of Usage and Career Benefits,' *Journal of Vocational Behavior* 118: 103396, doi: 10.1016/j.jvb.2020.103396

De Clerk, S. and Verreynne, M-L. (2017) 'The Networking Practices of Women Managers in an Emerging Economy Setting: Negotiating Institutional and Social Barriers,' *Human Resource Management Journal* 27(3): 477–501.

Dexter, B. and Wilson, M.G. (2017) *Making Your Net Work: Mastering the Art and Science of Career and Business Networking*, Chicago: Networlding Publishing.

Forret, M.L. and Dougherty, T.W. (2001) 'Correlates of Networking Behavior for Managerial and Professional Employees,' *Group & Organization Management* 26: 283–311.

Forret, M.L. and Dougherty, T.W. (2004) 'Networking Behaviors and Career Outcomes: Differences for Men and Women?' *Journal of Organizational Behavior* 25: 419–437.

Goldberg, L.R. (1990) 'An Alternative "Description of Personality": The Big-Five Factor Structure,' *Journal of Personality and Social Psychology* 59(6): 1216–1229.

Granovetter, M.S. (1970) *Changing Jobs: Channels of Mobility Information in a Suburban Community*. Doctoral dissertation. Harvard University.

Granovetter, M.S. (1973) 'The Strength of Weak Ties,' *American Journal of Sociology* 78(6): 1360–1380.

Granovetter, M.S. (1995) *Getting a Job: A Study of Contacts and Careers*, 2nd ed. Chicago: University of Chicago Press.

Gremmen, I., Akkerman, A. and Benscop, Y. (2013) 'Does Where You Stand Depend on How You Behave? Networking Behavior as an Alternative Explanation for Gender Differences in Network Structure,' *Journal of Management and Organization* 19(3): 297–313.

Ibarra, H., Kilduff, M. and Tsai, W. (2005) 'Zooming In and Out: Connecting Individuals and Collectivities at the Frontiers of Organizational Network Research,' *Organization Science* 16: 359–371.

Ibarra, H., Carter, N. and Silva, C. (2010) 'Why Men Still Get More Promotions Than Women,' *Harvard Business Review* 126: 80–85.

Kim, S. (2013) 'Networking Enablers, Constraints and Dynamics: A Qualitative Analysis,' *Career Development International* 18(2): 120–138.

Kožuh, I., Hinternair, M., Holzinger, A., Volčič, Z. and Debevc, M. (2015) 'Enhancing Universal Access: Deaf and Hard of Hearing People on Social Networking Sites,' *Universal Access in the Information Society* 14: 537–545.

McGuire, G.M. (2012) 'Race, Gender, and Social Support: A Study of Networks in a Financial Services Organization,' *Sociological Focus* 45: 320–337.

Milgram, S. (1967) 'The Small World Problem,' *Psychology Today* 2: 60–67.

142 Networking and personal growth

Mitra, J. and Basit, A. (2019) 'Personal Networks and Growth Aspirations: A Case Study of Second-Generation, Muslim, Female Entrepreneurs,' *Small Business Economics* 56(1): 121–143, https://doi.org/10.1007/s11187-019-00211-3

Peters, T. (1987) *Thriving on Chaos: Handbook for a Management Revolution*, New York: Alfred A. Knopf.

Peters, T. (1999) *Reinventing Work: The Brand You 50*, Toronto: Knopf, Random House.

Redler, M. (ed.) (2020) *Yearn, Earn, Learn: Expanding Your Horizons through Business Networking*, New York: Step Ahead Networking LLC.

Romero, C.C. (2018) 'Personal and Business Networks within Chilean Biotech,' *Industry and Innovation* 25(9): 841–873.

Ryan, R.M. and Deci, E.L. (2000) 'Self-Determination Theory and the Facilitation of Intrinsic Motivation, Social Development, and Well Being,' *American Psychologist* 55(1): 68–78.

Socratous, M. (2018) 'Networking: A Male Dominated Game,' *Gender in Management – An International Journal* 33(2): 167–183.

Thomas, S. (2016) *Instant Networking: The Simple Way to Build Your Business Network and See Results in Just 6 Months*, Chichester: John Wiley and Sons.

Van Den Brink, M. and Benschop, Y. (2014) 'Gender in Academic Networking: The Role of Gatekeepers in Professorial Recruitment,' *Journal of Management Studies* 51(3): 460–492, doi: 10.1111/joms.12060

Wolff, H.G. and Kim, S. (2012) 'The Relationship between Networking Behaviours and the Big Five Personality Dimensions,' *Career Development International* 17(1): 43–66, doi: 10.1108/13620431211201328.

INDEX

AIDS activism 97
Ansell, C. 57
Aristotle 34–36, 46
authenticity 40

Capra, F. 23
Castells, M. 23–24, 26, 54
civic engagement 99
co-creation 63, 102, 105
Colbertism 56
collaborative governance v. governing
collaboration 62
community of practice 12–15
counterculture 96
Critical Race Theory 139
cronyism 32

dialogue theory 106
Dougherty, T.W. 77, 131

elevator pitch 89, 92
empirical research 2, 17–18;
ethics approval 2
exchange theory 81

Facebook 102
Fem-Net-CA 27
first steps 137–139
Forret, M.L. 77, 131
freemasons 11

Gash, A. 57
gatekeeping 131–132

getting started 137–139
the Golden Rule 37
Granovetter, M. 16, 25, 119, 123
groupthink 43
guanxi 45

Halinen, N. 7, 24, 60, 83, 85, 86, 92
Health Innovation and Education Clusters
(HIECs) 55–67
heterophily 21, 45, 130
homophily 21, 43, 130, 131

inclusion and exclusion 43
in-crowding 19, 44, 126, 132
influence 20, 85, 98
innovation 20, 25, 53, 56–68, 82, 85, 121
innovation, social 96, 110
insight 20, 97, 126
instrumentality 36
intelligence 19, 85
International Baby Food Action Network
(IBFAN) 33
interpretation 20, 68

Kant, I. 37–40, 47
knowledge collectives 14
Kotter, J. 79

Lave, J. 13
LinkedIn 42, 125, 140
Linstone, H. 108

marketing perspectives 81–86

144 Index

mentoring 97, 122, 136
Milgram, S. 121
Mintzberg, H. 83
Möller, K. 7, 24, 60, 83, 85, 86, 92
mutuality 15–17

network-IN model 19, 68
networking: contagion 21; definition of
8, 78; effectiveness 26, 64, 65; ethics 25,
31–51; and friendship 34, 126; gender
in 131–134; internal 89–91; like/unlike,
relationships in 21, 98; motivation for 97,
134–136; outcomes 17–22, 63; power
33, 102, 111; specialist v. generalist 25;
strategic capability 86–88; principal
exclusions 8; and technology 23, 98
networks: formal 22, 53, 80; governance
61–62; leadership 60, 107; managed 53,
72; old boys 45; peer led 107, referrals
32; stakeholder management 67–72

personality types 128
Peters, T. 137
portfolio careers 137
privacy 40–42
professional bodies 11, 73

radical civic transitions 104
reciprocity 15–17, 21, 32, 98, 100, 101, 119,
128, 137
relationship marketing 81, 93
resistance to change 96, 136
resource–based view 86–87

self-consistency theory 100
self-determination theory 134–136
self-help books 137–139
self-help groups 102
silo working 91
six degrees of separation 121
Slack 27
SOC-ACT checklist 49, 112–113
social change model 114
stakeholder salience 71

task and finish groups 13
trade associations 11

unconscious bias 44, 114

Waters, J.A. 83
Wenger, E. 13
wicked problems 100

Printed in the United States
by Baker & Taylor Publisher Services